ONLY

THE

BEST

ONLY THE HE BEST

SIX QUALITIES
OF EXCELLENCE

BY
Edmund
Wallace Hildick

Clarkson N. Potter, Inc./Publisher NEW YORK

Printed in the United States of America

Library of Congress Catalog Card Number: 73-80336

ISBN: 0-517-505533

Published simultaneously in Canada by General Publishing Company Limited. Inquiries should be addressed to Clarkson N. Potter, Inc., 419 Park Avenue South, New York, N.Y., 10016.

First Edition

Designed by Ruth Smerechniak

Acknowledgements

Contents

ONLY
THE
BEST

the qualities that make a star out of an individual, taking him as far ahead of the field of regular talented coprofessionals as these are ahead of the lay public? That question is at the root of the present study.

At first sight, the word "professional" would seem to offer a rough-and-ready answer. We often talk of somebody's being "a true pro" or "a real pro" or having "the professional touch" when we really mean that the individual in question has turned in a superlative performance, or is in the habit of doing so—quite forgetting that the opponent he has just danced rings around or the colleague who has supported him is also a true professional in the sense that he is good enough to make a living out of what he has a talent for, and is even sufficiently competent to enter the same arena as our hero. And if one is more than a spectator or consumer—if one has some direct interest in a certain body of professionals, as a promoter, say, or publisher or impresario, then the term "a true pro," expressed with perhaps rather more gratification than admiration, can mean something else again. It can mean, for instance, a good reliable hack, someone who doesn't make waves, who obeys instructions, who never pulls hair-raising surprises, who is, in short, lacking in some of the very qualities that go to make so many (but not all) stars.

Then again there is the commendatory use of the word "professional" often made by the pros themselves, when speaking in effect of "a pro's pro"—a writers' writer, say, or a football players' football player. This isn't what we're after either, since so often it has the backhanded connotation associated with that more general term "a man's man" (who, it is implied, can't always get along with women). Thus a writers' writer is often one who fails to make the highest grade, perhaps because of a penchant for injudicious experiment, who is little known to the general public, and whose work can therefore be borrowed from with relative impunity.

§ 2 §

Similarly, a football players' football player often turns out to be a technically gifted but unlucky or unenterprising (same thing?) stiff who can be cited when the applause for some envied unquestionable star starts getting unendurable.

An interesting multiple example of this overlapping and blurring of definitions occurs in Saul Bellow's *Henderson the Rain King*. When King Dahfu takes part in a ritual skull-tossing game, Henderson's reactions are as to watching "a fine tennis player or a great rider" because although the king's confidence seemed great, "and his bounding and his quick turns and his sureness made beautiful watching . . . and he—well, he was virile to a degree that made all worry superfluous; such a man takes all he does upon himself; nevertheless I trembled and shook for him." In other words, Dahfu was displaying the qualities of a certain type of super-pro by introducing an element beyond skill—something that I once heard a jazz musician (I think it was Brubeck) describe as a kind of tightrope walker's spellbinding power—a constant stretching of technical resources to a point just short of disaster. One may be sure that the managers and promoters of such stars are too busy mopping their foreheads and hunting around for insurance to lavish the term "a real pro" on them, just as, indeed, Dahfu's tribal elders frowned on his (to them) unnecessarily highly risky practice of spending hours every day locked in a cellar with a lioness so that he could absorb the very essence of the species into his whole being before undertaking the hunt that was to be his supreme trial. Later in the book, however, when Bellow has Henderson directly refer to the king's professionalism— "You are bred for this; you are a pro. If there's anything I love to see, it's a guy who's good at his work. Whether it's a rigger or steeplejack or window-washer or any person who has strong nerves and a skilled body"—he seems to be using the term merely as a layman's compliment to a skill or talent he doesn't himself possess.

Nevertheless, despite all this confusion, there is still something about the word "professional" that seems to offer a key and merits our staying with it a while longer. According to the Oxford English Dictionary, English-speaking humanity would appear to have been inching its way toward some deeper, acclamatory use of the word for centuries. Starting with Saint Etheldred, we find it used in a strictly technical sense, pertaining to entry into a religious order. ("Hit was hurre professhennalle rynge.") Later it came into use—again as a straight descriptive term—to relate to the so-called learned professions: medicine, divinity, and the law —as well as the military. Only in the nineteenth century did a certain emotional coloring creep in, with here a note of rather petty pride ("I dislike doing anything professional in private parties"—1838) and there a note of rather petty contempt ("As perfectly professional as the mourning of an undertaker"—1870); and for a time this pejorative tendency increased with the widening usage of the word to denote a paid performer as against an amateur, gifted or otherwise. So there came into currency the term *"professional beauty . . .* humorously applied to a lady with the implication that she makes it her business to be a beauty, or to be known as such"—and with it the huffing and puffing of one set of politicians calling another "professionals," again in the words of the O.E.D.: "disparagingly applied to one who 'makes a trade' of anything that is properly pursued from higher motives." Nowadays of course it is the term "amateur" that more often comes with the sneer, as a synonym for "sloppy" —though there must have been uneasy doubts about the efficacy of higher motives alone, even in 1882, for the *Boys' Own Paper* to confess that "our amateurs are improving, and the interval between them and the professionals is growing beautifully less." Presumably this referred to cricket, in which sport the professionals generally continued to have the edge over the amateurs right into the middle of the present century, when at last the official distinction (and the segregated locker rooms that went with it) was mercifully abandoned.

But apart from such shifts in the range of petty abuse, the O.E.D. registers another usage that came into prominence in the nineteenth century and (together with the Saint Etheldred quotation and its hint at dedication) it might turn out to be far more pertinent to our inquiry. Here is the New Professional, defined as one

that is trained and skilled in the theoretic or scientific parts of a trade or occupation, as distinct from its merely mechanical parts; that raises his trade to the dignity of a learned profession

—a definition charmingly supported by a quotation from the *Westminster Gazette* of 18 January 1898: "A witness described himself as a professional gardener . . . 'There is a vast difference between professional and ordinary gardeners. I am competent to give a lecture on botany and horticulture.' "

CABBAGES AND KINGS (AND A PRINCESS)

The gardener, it should be noted, does not mention remuneration. In fact it would make no difference to his definition whether or not he was paid for his erudite labors. Similarly, the question of payment is no barrier to our recognition of a quality that could be called professional in this sense when considering championship-class individuals in areas that are exclusively or almost exclusively the province of amateurs— athletics, for example. To shine there, to prove one's supremacy, to test one's talent and skills against the best, one simply has to be an amateur—a nonprofessional in the narrow sense of those terms. But when the Russian trainer Valentin Petrovsky says this, of his crack running pupil, Borzov—"He has the perfect temperament. He does not get excited. He does not look forward or backward. He exists in the moment. He does not think about the race he is running until he approaches the starting line. Then he remembers everything he has learned, and his tensions are exactly right. He can concentrate without fear—and that is what makes a great athlete in competition"—why, then Petrovsky is talking about professionalism, or, rather, about superprofessionalism in the deeper sense. *"He can concentrate without fear."* We must remember that.

Meanwhile (still on the subject of Olympics-type athletics), Princess Anne of England seemed to be getting close to the heart of the question, albeit by accident, when, at the opening of a national sports center in Wales, she spoke of "that moment in sport when the enjoyment wears off because of the pressure put on you to be successful." Here we have not only a definition of the difference between the everyday nonchampionship class amateur and professional, but also between the everyday professional and the superpro. For in practice the enjoyment factor carries over into this rarer atmosphere. It may not be enjoyment of the weather, or the smell of grass, or the feel of salt spray, or the tea with strawberries and cream, or the jolly good fellowship of one's colleagues and competitors. But if there is one thing common to all stars it is their enjoyment of *success* itself. What is more, they enjoy it so much (are in fact addicted to it) that they'll put up with much more hardship, sacrifice, and deprivation than the regular hack pros.

An interesting gloss is thrown on the Princess's somewhat stereotyped remarks, however, when it is realized that she was speaking in the context of some introductory paean by Lieutenant-Colonel Harry Llewellyn, himself an Olympic gold medalist for show jumping, who had referred to her "brilliant achievements in riding." She thanked him, but added: "I would like to think that one day I shall be as successful." Given the logistics of success in such a competitive field—the need for single-mindedness and all the other factors, some of which we have touched on already, and all of which we shall be examining in detail later—and given her own good sense, there was clearly more wistfulness than confidence in that wish. Even so, as a *princess*—and a princess who is sufficiently on top of her job to be aware how little the old Elizabethan pour-it-on-thick type of flattery counts with the public these days, and how much plain common sense is valued in a royal—her gentle brushing aside of the gallant colonel's compliment must earn her points for superprofessionalism in her own field.

But to return to our proud gardener. He also gives us a pointer to another aspect of the subject, and it is this: professionalism—superprofessionalism—is not confined to such glamour activities as sports and the arts, politics, and jazz. We must talk of cabbages as well as of kings. Even garbage, if it comes to that.

Yes. Garbage.

There appeared on a British Broadcasting Corporation news program not long ago a Mr. Allen, Chief Public Health Inspector of Scunthorpe, Lincolnshire, who by any reckoning is worthy of joining the ranks of the superpros. For he is not content to apply to the problem of garbage disposal a clinical proficiency in the ordinary professional sense, regarding it as a somewhat unpleasant but necessary job that one is paid to get done as well as can be expected. Instead, he has obviously grown to cherish its challenges, meeting them with an enthusiasm, even a gusto, that transforms mere efficiency (and Scunthorpe is one of the few municipalities in the country actually to show a profit in the field) into a resounding repeated victory. His is the kind of positiveness and totality of engagement that one finds in so many of the great professionals in more exalted arenas. He experiments: not only with various methods of crushing and compounding the waste products of the township, of dumping them tidily and safely, and of getting things to grow out of them. Many Public Health Officers are doing that sort of thing nowadays. But Mr. Allen is forever seeking fresh, less obvious uses, like the manufacture of a new kind of building block out of broken glass, an experiment that he confesses, with the equanimity of the truly dedicated superpro who knows he will succeed in time, is still not wholly successful. What is more, in all this he has managed to sustain a feeling for the less obviously useful aspects of the work—the sense of joy that some would put down as mere frivolity, but which many great professionals, particularly in the arts, know well can lead to major discoveries. Mr. Allen's working model of the municipal dump, for instance, might be regarded by some as an engaging schoolboyish indulgence, just as they might feel that his building up of a museum of curiosities found in the garbage is a charming, rather cranky sideshow and nothing else. But who are they to say—lacking the fire of the superpro's enthusiasm—what significant by-products of the creative imagination might not be cast up at such paranormal temperatures? Picasso himself might have had a thing or two to tell them on that score.

But now let us take a look at the relationship of superprofessionalism to garbage of a different kind. Quite a stir was made in Mafia circles recently by a shooting that was alleged to have taken place at a New Year's party, when a waiter and waitress were killed. In the course of the ensuing prosecution the following conversation was said to have been overheard—between the Mafia soldier accused of the crime and one of his superiors, who had not been present at the incident. Indeed, so superior was this latter in more than rank—the nature of his comments will soon make this clear —and so inferior the former that instead of using their actual names it will perhaps be more pertinent to this inquiry to designate them as Superpro and Mere Pro.

Superpro begins by asking what happened.

MERE PRO: I don't know. I blew my top. This black bastard was arguing and dancing with one of my relatives, drinking and getting rumbustious. I told him this is not your party, you're here to serve and not to mingle with the people. The black guy said to me, don't give me no mouth, and started arguing. I blew my top. I shot the guy.

SUPERPRO: What did you do with the girl? [The waitress, the dead man's girl friend.]

MERE PRO: I went and reloaded.

SUPERPRO: What do you mean, while the girl stood there you went and reloaded?

MERE PRO: Yeah, then I shot the girl.

Presumably while Superpro was recovering from shock at this confession of sloppiness, Mere Pro went on to explain that he and some of his friends then took the bodies and dumped them. By "friends" he was apparently referring to everyday, off-duty, nonprofessional buddies, for the Superpro was quick to point out that he should have called on the assistance only of Mafia friends, and *buried,* not merely dumped, the corpses; whereupon the other again admitted he'd slipped up. Then he asked for guidance.

§ 9 §

SUPERPRO: Your main problem is how you are going to keep all those people down. You can't trust your own in-laws, you can't kill them all. You should burn the house down.

Wise after the event, Mere Pro agreed that this would be a good way of destroying some of the evidence at least; while his mentor, so gripped by the technicalities as to have forgotten his earlier surprise and annoyance, continues in a higher strategic vein.

SUPERPRO: I know the chief of police out there. I probably could get in touch with the judge, but it will cost you.

MERE PRO: I'll go as high as a hundred thousand dollars.

Sickening though this conversation might be in its content, it does give some remarkably vivid insights into the subject of our inquiry. Note, for instance, Superpro's clinical interest in a problem that must have caused such acute embarrassment in his circle. Contrast his *thinking* posture with the other's almost childish lack of thought in the first instance. ("I don't know. I blew my top.") Note too his dedication to his calling, a dedication that would presumably have allowed him to go ahead and kill his own near relatives if this would have helped to correct the mistake. And note his grasp of concrete practicalities—his refusal to rage over unnecessarily and dangerously spilled blood, and his concern to repair the damage as quickly and effectively as possible. There is no record of his then having proceeded to draw for the other Lessons to Be Learned from the Catastrophe, but if he's the kind of pro the rest of the conversation proclaims him to be one could put a safe bet on it. As for Mere Pro, it seems a pity for all concerned that he should never have read, and taken to heart, the words of Dickens's Miss Petowker of the Theatre Royal Drury Lane, requoted here earlier from the O.E.D.: "...I dislike doing anything professional in private parties."

THE STAR IN THE STREET

It is fashionable nowadays in some circles to sneer at professionalism of the kind we have been discussing—at the drive to do, and the doing of, anything superlatively well—but even here, at the very heart of antiprofessionalism, there have to be men and women who approach their revolutionary tasks with all the verve and determination, the dedication and the thoroughness, of the superstar. An interesting sidelight on this is thrown by the following extract from the official transcript of the trial of the so-called Chicago Seven:

Chicago Policewoman Mary Ellen Dahl: And he said that "We're going to storm the Hilton. We can't make it without weapons. We are going to need a lot of weapons, so we should bring rocks, bottles, sticks, and another good weapon is a brick. But we have to break the bricks in half so that it will be easier to conceal and it will be easier to throw and the girls can throw them too," and then he asked if anybody had any suggestions or ideas on other weapons, and someone in the group behind me said, "Yes. We should take the bottles and break them in half because if we throw broken bottles they are going to do more damage broken than whole," and he said, "Yeah, that's a good idea." And he said, "Another good idea is golf balls with—"
Q. Who said, "Another good idea is golf balls"?
A. Hoffman said, "Another good idea is golf balls, with nails pounded through them at all different angles, so that when you throw them, they will stick," and he said, "But don't forget the vaseline for your faces to protect against the MACE, because there's going to be a lot of MACE flying . . ."

Whatever we may think about the merits or demerits of the case, or the reliability of the various statements made during the trial, we have in this extract an excellent example of the difference between the workings of the expert's mind and the amateur's: the meticulous attention to detail on the one hand, and the slapdash, headlong, suggestion-born impulse on the other. The expert has three good reasons for breaking bricks, but the amateur's suggestion seems to be based on nothing more than the mere follow-my-leader pattern of "if breaking bricks is a good idea, so must breaking bottles be"—after which he sticks on the pseudoreason: "They are going to do more damage." In fact, as any veteran street fighter could have told him, whole bottles are easier to throw, are infinitely more accurate if thrown the proper way, have a double chance of doing damage by acting as stunning missiles on impact as well as cutting and fragmentary missiles after impact, are easier to conceal without doing the carrier an injury, and are simpler to explain away if one is caught in possession of them. Certainly the expert may have said to the booby, "Yeah, that's a good idea"—but only in his role as tutor, much as any good teacher will give such praise in passing if he feels the recipient's interest or enthusiasm for the subject deserves encouraging.

Another good example of superprofessionalism appearing in a sphere not usually associated with such qualities is to be found in Piri Thomas's autobiography, *Down These Mean Streets*. As a kid, Thomas discovered that it was as tough to keep ahead of one's competitors at the bottom, shining shoes, as it is for any movie actor at the top. "It was hard to shine shoes and harder to keep my corner from getting copped by an early-rising shine boy. I had to be prepared to mess a guy up; that corner spot wasn't mine alone." Yet the strong-arm tactics weren't by any means sufficient in themselves, as the boy was bright enough to realize. "I had to earn it every time I shined shoes there." Here is his account of the service he provided:

When I got a customer, we both played our roles. The customer, tall and aloof, smiled, "Gimme a shine, kid," and I replied, *"Sì, señor,* sir, I'll give you one that you'll have to put sunglasses on to eat the bright down."

My knees grinding against the gritty sidewalk, I adopted a serious, businesslike air. Carefully, but confidently, I snaked out my rags, polish, and brushes. I gave my cool breeze customer the treatment. I rolled his pants cuff up—"That'll keep the polish off"—straightened his socks, patted his shoe, assured him he was in good hands, and loosened and retied his shoes. Then I wiped my nose with a delicate finger, picked up my shoe brush, and scrunched away the first hard crust of dirt. I opened my bottle of black shoe cleaner—dab, rub in, wipe off, pat the shoe down. Then I opened my can of polish—dab on with three fingers, pat-a-pid, pat-a-pid. He's not looking—spit on the shoe, more polish, let it dry, tap the bottom of the sole, smile up at Mr. Big Tip (you hope), "Next, sir."

I repeated the process on the other shoe, then picked up my brush and rubbed the bristles very hard against the palm of my hand, scientific-like, to warm the brush hairs up so they would melt the black shoe wax and give a cool unlumpy shine. I peeked out of the corner of my eye to see if Mr. Big Tip was watching my modern shoe-shine methods. The bum *was* looking. I hadn't touched his shoe, forcing him to look.

The shoe began to gleam dully—more spit, more polish, more brush, little more spit, little more polish, and a lotta rag. I repeated on the other shoe. As Mr. Big Tip started digging in his pocket, I prepared for the climax of my performance. Just as he finished saying, "Damn nice shine, kid," I said, "Oh, I ain't finished, sir. I got a special service," and I plunged my wax-covered fingers into a dark corner of my shoe box and brought out a bottle of "Special shoe lanolin cream for better preservation of the leather."

I applied a dab, a tiny dab, pausing long enough to say very confidently, "You can't put on too much of it or it'll spoil the shine. It gotta be just right." Then I grabbed the shoe rag firmly, like a maestro with a baton, and hummed a rhythm with it, slapping out a happy beat on the shoes. A final swish here and there, and *mira!*—finished. Sweating from the effort of my creation, I slowly rose from my knees, bent from the strain, my hand casually extended, palm flat up, and murmured, "Fifteen cents, sir," with a look that said, "But it's worth much more, don't you think?" Mr. Big Tip dropped a quarter and a nickel into the offering plate, and I said, "Thanks a mil, sir," thinking, *Take it cool,* as I cast a watchful eye at his retreating back.

But wasn't it great to work for a living? I calculated how long it would take to make my first million shining shoes. Too long. I would be something like 987 years old. Maybe I could steal it faster.*

It will probably have been seen that in this last extract we have two streams of expertise: the confidence trickster's as well as the shoeshiner's. But in each case the subject approaches the task with the application, the thoughtfulness (all angles, every side), and the meticulous attention to detail of superpros in more exalted fields. As the book goes on to show, this quality of approach suffered a disastrous falling off when Thomas did turn to stealing, culminating in a hopelessly bungled nightclub stickup that earned him a near-fatal bullet wound and several years in prison. But then, his heart couldn't really have been in that kind of work, and the assiduity and gusto of the shoe-cleaning, sweet-talking, prestigious interlude wasn't to reappear again with anything like the same force until he began to exercise his late-discovered talent as a writer. Ample evidence is to be found in *Down These Mean Streets,* and nowhere so markedly as in the

---

* Piri Thomas, *Down These Mean Streets.*

meticulousness with which the slang expressions (ranging from the early 1930s to the mid-forties) are orchestrated, so that while no word is out of place on the time scale the smoothness of the narrative flow is maintained: a quite remarkable achievement in a first book, even when it is remembered that Thomas had the help of an equally meticulous and sensitive editor in Angus Cameron of Knopf.

ELEMENTS OF SUPERPROFESSIONALISM

But now that we are back with superprofessionalism in one of its more generally recognized contexts—having noted that in reality there are scarcely any restrictions on its areas of operation—it would be useful to take stock, to try to draw from the examples already quoted whatever common or frequently recurring elements there might happen to be, and to see if any firm pattern can be traced and subsequently examined in detail.

Even in so short a space these elements have proved to be numerous. They include: dedication; total commitment; total interest; hunger for success; passionate enthusiasm; willingness to accept responsibility (for the talent and its highest exercises); a thoroughness in application that embraces and is often built on theoretical research; a pride in achievement; a power of concentration; an ability to think strategically as well as tactically; great cunning; a willingness to experiment and a readiness to learn—and borrow; a willingness to instruct and pass on one's expertise (a desire to extend one's career beyond the physical termination point?); a willingness to recognize one's mistakes (if only in private), so that they may be analysed and eradicated; an eagerness to analyze the mistakes of others; a readiness to take enormous (but always calculated) risks; control of emotions and general self-discipline; courage; close attention to detail; and self-confidence.

Some of these do of course tend to overlap and cluster. Thus the dedication, total commitment, and so on, may conveniently be grouped under the general head of *Single-mindedness*, for which success-hunger, enthusiasm, and pride in achievement all provide the power. Some require further exegesis to become meaningful, like that bland old cliché self-confidence, which is only really tested under conditions of defeat or disappointment or the discovery of flaws (otherwise it lurches into the trap of overconfidence and becomes the undoing of so many would-be superpros). Similarly courage, if it is not to be confused with rashness—another great pitfall—must be examined in the context of the subject's fears and anxieties, and his ability to control them. And again, the group involving willingness to experiment, the urge to accumulate knowledge and so on, must be seen in its practical aspect—in the superpro's drive toward the perfection of his skills, toward making the very best of his talent. As for attention to detail, it enters into every part of the subject, yet is so important that it surely deserves a category of its own; for while no one can become a superpro with only an infinite capacity for taking pains to his credit, without a *respect* for detail any other quality he possesses will never become sufficiently developed.

Here then, as the basis for further examination, with an emphasis on the practicality that is the essence of the subject, are the six qualities I should propose when answering the question about what sorts the stars from the ruck of talented but only moderately competent practitioners or performers:

1. Single-mindedness
2. An ability to make the very best of the material at hand

3. An ability to handle mistakes
4. An ability to control (and use) one's emotions
5. An ability to survive defeat and disappointment
6. Attention to detail

Whether a superpro needs the whole battery, or whether an individual can make it with only five, four, three, or even two of these qualities is a supplementary question we can expect to be in a better position to answer at the end.

2

Single-Mindedness

LAYING UP TREASURES

Whether one admires it as dedication or vilifies it as monstrous egotism, one is bound to recognize that single-mindedness is probably the most valuable ingredient in a superpro's makeup. Powered by morally suspect elements like pride and hunger for success, it in turn generates such clean, generally approved and vitally important by-products as enthusiasm, persistence, power of concentration, and prodigious industry. Yet it is rarely, if ever, a given state. It does not come with the talent, prepacked and ready to go. It has to be worked on, arranged, built up, maintained, protected, cosseted.

In other words, in the life of any potentially great professional, provision must be made systematically against encroachments and distractions, particularly distractions of a nature normally considered unavoidable, like recurring economic needs, family demands, and the acquisition of the very means to remain alive and talented and living in hope. Money, in sufficient quantities, can do much to help cut down these day-to-day bread-and-butter distractions as well as keep under control the more exotic ones deriving from a taste for luxuries or indulgence in expensive habits, but only so long as the getting of the money doesn't itself encroach too much on the time that should be devoted to the cultivation and perfection of one's skills, and to their sustained exercise.

Sinecures used to be a big help in certain spheres, as did direct financial patronage, functions taken over today by the fellowship and the scholarship. But again these are effective only so long as the lobbying or ass-crawling or letter writing or defensive politicking involved doesn't become a liability on one's time and energy. Self-subsidy—the prudent laying up of treasures made during certain well-timed working sabbatical breaks in a professional's career, or before fully embarking on it, or by shrewd and thorough financial milking of whatever successes may have come along the way—is another method. Unfortunately for the would-be superpro, it is so tricky as to constitute an extra profession and one that is better handled (in its concurrent aspects at least) by a good manager, who in turn deserves and usually requires a good salary or fee. On the other hand, a sufficiently determined professional might decide to tackle the problem from the consumption angle, by training himself to live frugally, or by setting up his base where the costs are very low, or, as many have done, by dispensing with his sense of responsibility toward any family he might have, or by avoiding such entanglements from the outset. Or, again as many have done, he might choose to indulge in and enjoy to the full all such extraprofessional activities, respectable or otherwise, and get away with the minimum of distraction simply by welshing on his bills or relying on some other form of illegality to provide the money for paying them. (Though this too has its limitations, where criminality itself becomes a conflicting profession, with its own set of demands—and even menaces.) A third way, coming somewhere between the last two, is to create a kind of do-it-yourself sinecure, taking a job that pays reasonably well and then doing as little for that money as possible. Here again, however, there are built-in penalties, for to do this really effectively and continue to get away with it is an art in itself, so that the conflict of interests becomes great enough to produce another major crop of distractions. People naturally endowed with thick skins and well-compartmentalized consciences are most likely to succeed in this last method, which is possibly, nowadays, the most popular. And—since talents themselves don't necessarily come singly —there must have been many a switch along this line, as on the others described, where the budding violinist or writer or painter has turned superpro businessman, or thief, and taken this new career to starry heights. (Even superpro panhandler. Some of the world's greatest exponents of this art now operate in Manhattan: educated kids who have brought to the job all the methods of modern business psychology, and who make the old-time European and Asian pro beggars seem like so many weekend actors and actresses, for all their tricksy stumps and open sores and so forth.)

From all this, it is not difficult to see how the various romantic clichés have come into being: the starving in garrets, for example, and the high-handed ruthless egotism of the Artist, so often embarked upon or indulged in by those without the talent to be supported and stupid enough to think that the starving or people-trampling is in itself a recipe for eventual professional success. The trouble with the garret thing was that it came into prominence on the flood tide of Romanticism and was almost indelibly stained by it. But to the garret-starvers of that era—the Renoirs and Pissarros and Monets—this was no amusing affectation or some mystical ascetic source of inspiration. To the contrary, it was a sheer nitty-gritty economic necessity, theirs being a revolutionary type of art in an age when whatever patronage was forthcoming in the field was usually confined, along with the taste of the paying public, to conservative paintings. So these men were desperately short of money, with all the bodily demands likely to cause serious distraction if unfulfilled. So they set up studios where the living was cheapest—always commensurate with their basic cultural needs—which meant bumming along and pooling resources in some poor quarter of a big, adequately galleried city. So they survived and concentrated on their art. It is significant that those of their contemporaries who could squeeze moderate allowances from parents or other relatives did so and, like Cézanne, generally chose to live in more salubrious (meaning more peaceful, less distracting) surroundings.

But man—the budding superpro as well as nice ordinary reasonably well-adjusted man—doesn't live by bread alone. He needs companionship, affection, recreation, and so on, and here again, especially in the give-and-take field of human relationships, certain individuals find the attendant distractions too much if they are to devote enough attention to their talents. Hence the phenomenon of the sycophant, the traveling yes-circus, in the lives of many highly successful superpros. We should really spare a little more sympathy than we do for such leeches, because although it may be a matter of calculated greed on their part, the subject's role is rarely that of a mere passive victim. Far from it. The star, like any other human, does need to a greater or lesser degree the companionship of other humans—*but only when it fits in with the demands of his talent.* Otherwise, the give-and-take of friendship, the stopping by and the keeping of dates, the lending a hand and the offering of the tear-absorbing shoulder, escalates from being a mere nuisance to a positive threat. With bought friends—the pro buddies—there is no need to stand on ceremony. When the successful superpro himself needs a shoulder to cry on, or a boon companion to celebrate with, or simply someone to talk to during a bout of insomnia, he just snaps his fingers, whistles, or picks up the phone. Similarly, when a new professional idea strikes him in the middle of one of his own parties, he need spare no feelings in showing such companions the door. In fact sycophancy at this level can be a highly skilled profession in itself, with its own superpros—and one that has almost as valuable a contribution to make to mankind as the talents of the stars it services.

PORTRAIT OF THE ARTIST AS A YOUNG SNOT

But how is the problem handled by the emergent superpro, or the superpro who is so far financially unsuccessful? Again the solution might lie in deliberate self-denial, in training oneself to do without the pleasures of friendship, even in geographical retreat to the hills or the proverbial desert island, especially when the talent to be developed with single-minded assiduity is one that can be exercised in solitude, like painting. More often, however, it is an untidy psychological retreat, wherein the subject makes *himself* into an island—craggy, bare, forbidding—by surly or quarrelsome or frightening behavior.

Such a case seems to have been Cézanne's. "Isolation is

what I am worthy of," he once wrote. "Thus, at least, no one gets me in his clutches." And, consciously or subconsciously, he saw to it that this isolation was preserved by the frequent sudden brusque treatment of old friends and new well-wishers alike. John Rewald, in his biography of the painter, quotes the following characteristic incident, involving a young artist with whom Cézanne had struck up a friendship not of his own seeking, the young man having been encouraged to visit him by an old friend who should have known better.

Cézanne had asked his young colleague to call him every day at three o'clock after his nap; Le Bail, taking him at his word, and finding Cézanne asleep, entered his room after having knocked several times to wake him. The next day Louis Le Bail received this letter:

> "*Monsieur:*
> "*The rather discourteous manner with which you take the liberty of entering my room is not calculated to please me. In the future please see that you are announced. Please give the glass and the canvas which were left in your studio to the person who comes for them.*"*

A clearer case of the engineering of an early break of relations it would be hard to find, unless it be the incident in which he gave the brush-off to a much older friend, Francisco Oller. Meeting the latter in Paris after many years, Cézanne began with what was doubtlessly a genuine warm impulse by inviting Oller to accompany him to his home town of Aix, agreeing to meet at the third-class carriages of a certain train. Duly arrived at the station, however, Oller was unable to find Cézanne, and so decided to wait for the next train—

---

* This and subsequent quotations about the artist are from John Rewald's *Paul Cézanne.*

little realizing that Cézanne had taken a first-class compartment on the earlier one. In spite of this shot across the bows of his friendship (for that surely is what it was, intentionally or otherwise), Oller persisted, going on to stay in Aix for a couple of weeks. There he regularly visited Cézanne until at last he gave the painter the opportunity his instincts had been waiting for by venturing to proffer Cézanne advice on painting, thereby calling down on his head this letter:

Sir,
The high-handed manner you have adopted toward me for some time and the rather brusque tone you permitted yourself to use, at the moment you took leave, are not calculated to please me.
I am determined not to receive you in my father's house. The lessons that you take the liberty of giving me will thus have borne their fruits. Goodbye.
P. Cézanne.

Nobody was immune from the consequences of this instinct for self-protection; not even Emile Zola, the painter's oldest and best friend, who received a brush-off letter commensurate with his status—subtler but no less clear in its implications:

My dear Emile,
I have just received L'Oeuvre [in which Cézanne felt himself to have been unsympathetically treated through the persona of the painter-hero of the novel] *which you were good enough to send me. I thank the author of* Les Rougon-Macquart *for this kind token of remembrance and ask him to permit me to clasp his hand while thinking of bygone years.*
Ever yours under the impulse of past times.
Paul Cézanne.

Remembrance, bygone years, and the final whipcrack of "under the impulse of past times"—all these added up to one thing, and Zola well knew it. The two men never met again, even though the novelist lived on for another sixteen years.

But it was Zola who, in the earliest days of their friendship, had indirectly forecast its end by this remarkable portrait of the artist as embattled genius:

Proving something to Cézanne would be like trying to persuade the towers of Notre Dame to dance a quadrille. He might say yes, but he would not budge an inch. . . . Nothing bends him, nothing can force him to make a concession. He does not even want to discuss what he thinks; he abhors discussion, because to talk is tiring, and also because it would be necessary to change his opinion if his adversary were right. There he is, thrown into the middle of life, bringing with him certain ideas, unwilling to change them except on his own judgement, nevertheless the nicest fellow in the world, always agreeing with you. . . . [But] if, by chance, he advances a contrary opinion and you dispute it, he flies into a rage without wishing to examine, screams that you know nothing about the subject, and jumps to something else.

Frequently there need be no manufactured self-protective unpleasantness, conscious or otherwise, no friends to have to repel. Nature will have played a part right from birth or during early upbringing, endowing the talented individual with a sufficiently uncongenial personality—one that will in time, incidentally, prove a double benefit, ensuring that he is left much alone while at the same time generating creative power in the form of an urge to compensate by excelling in some special skill. Johannes Kepler, the mathematician, physicist, and founder of modern astronomy, began life as such a one, in the words of Arthur Koestler: "the neurotic child from a problem family, covered with scabs and boils, who feels that whatever he does is a pain to others and a disgrace to himself."* But far from allowing himself to be submerged in self-pity, Kepler "was a Job who shamed his Lord by making trees grow from his boils. In other words, he had that mysterious knack of finding original outlets for inner pressure, of transforming his torments into creative achievement..." And certainly, unlike many repulsive geniuses, Kepler had the irony and sense of humor to realize this, as the following passage, describing himself in the third person, as a young man and while still a young man, shows:

That man [himself] has in every way a doglike nature. His appearance is that of a little lap dog. . . . Even his appetites were alike: he liked gnawing bones and dry crusts of bread, and was so greedy that whatever his eyes chanced on he grabbed; yet, like a dog, he drinks little and is content with the simplest food. His habits were similar. . . . He is bored with conversation, but greets visitors just like a little dog; yet when the least thing is snatched away from him, he flares up and growls. He tenaciously persecutes wrongdoers—that is, he barks at them. He is malicious and bites people with his sarcasms. He hates many people exceedingly and they avoid him. . . . He has a doglike horror of baths, tinctures, and lotions.

Then there are cases where a superpro's personality, though congenial enough on the surface, possesses by nature a socially disastrous but professionally invaluable flaw—like James Joyce's almost pathological suspicion of treachery. This was a suspicion so strong that it often seemed to induce betrayal in others, thereby justifying his impulses toward that central element in his triple recipe for success: silence, exile, cunning. But Joyce was a great family man, it may be pointed out. At least his wife and children were never re-

* This and subsequent quotations regarding Kepler are from *The Watershed* by Arthur Koestler, a biography of Kepler abstracted from Koestler's *The Sleepwalkers*.

§ 27 §

jected or even neglected by him on their often harassing wanderings. Well, maybe not—on the surface of things. Joyce certainly was never stinting in his affection for them. But neither was there ever any question of sparing them the privations of those years of self-imposed exile. It seems to me that in this connection one of the most illuminating passages in Richard Ellmann's great biographical study of the novelist is the following:

As a father, Joyce wished to interfere as little as possible with his children's lives, a principle which was better suited to his own insuperable personality than to theirs. Because he rarely ordered or forbade them anything, and always treated them kindly and generously, he assumed they had their freedom. But by delicate requests, by sighs, by suggestions, he bound them into his affairs. They were slow to make their own careers.*

And elsewhere in the study Ellmann makes much the same point through an analysis of Joyce's self-reflecting hero, Stephen Dedalus, and the ties of his family and friends:

Although Stephen Dedalus . . . assumes his isolation, he surrounds himself with friends and family to whom he can confide it. When he rebels he hastens to let them know of his rebellion so that he can measure their response to it. He searches for disciples who must share his motives vicariously. As he demands increasing allegiance from them, step by step, he brings them to the point where they will go no further, and their refusal, half-anticipated, enables him to feel forsaken and to forsake them.

IN THEIR OWN SWEET WAY...

Another great family man, in a different, more boisterous key, was Charles Dickens, yet even he, for all his enormous

---

* This and later quotations are from Richard Ellmann's *James Joyce.*

energy, respected his talent enough, and the need for giving it pride of place in his attentions, to keep a wary eye on the dangers of too much interference, as the following extract from one of his letters testifies:

A necessity is upon me now—as at most times—of wandering about in my old wild way, to think. I could no more resist this on Sunday or yesterday than a man can dispense with food, or a horse can help himself from being driven. I hold my inventive capacity on the stern condition that it must master my whole life, often have complete possession of me, make its own demands upon me, and sometimes, for months together, put everything else away from me. If I had not known long ago that my place could never be held, unless I were at any moment ready to devote myself to it entirely, I should have dropped out of it very soon. All this I can hardly expect you to understand—or the restlessness and waywardness of an author's mind. You have never seen it before you, or lived with it, or had occasion to think or care about it, and you cannot have the necessary consideration for it. "It is only half-an-hour"—"It is only an afternoon"—"It is only an evening," people say to me over and over again; but they don't know that it is impossible to command one's self sometimes to any stipulated and set disposal of five minutes—or that the mere consciousness of an engagement will sometimes worry a whole day. These are the penalties paid for writing books. Whoever is devoted to an art must be content to deliver himself wholly up to it, and to find his recompense in it. I am grieved if you suspect me of not wanting to see you, but I can't help it; I must go my way whether or no.

Granted there might have been some foundation to the recipient's suspicions. The letter was to his old flame Maria Beadnell, the Dora of *David Copperfield,* who had reappeared in the author's middle life as Mrs. Henry Winter. But what he says is clearly more than an excuse to brush off someone he no longer cared about who threatened to become a general nuisance. He could write in almost exactly the same terms to so dear and valued a friend as Burdett Coutts, declining an invitation to one of her splendid dinner parties, explaining that he was "in agonies of plotting and contriving a new book,"

in which stage of the tremendous process, I am accustomed to walk up and down the house, smiting my forehead dejectedly; and to be so horribly cross and surly that the boldest fly at my approach. . . . Seriously, unless I were to shut myself up obstinately and sullenly in my room for a great many days without writing a word, I don't think I should ever make a beginning . . . the lapse of every new day only gives me stronger reasons for being perseveringly uncomfortable, that out of my gloom and solitude something comical, or meant to be, may straightway grow up.

We may be sure that what went for friends and old acquaintances went for the family too, especially when the professional squeeze was really on—which it regularly was, thanks to Dickens's habit of writing for periodical publication, with all its deadlines and sudden crises. As early in his relationship with Kate as a few weeks before their marriage he was telling her—or trying to tell her—where it was at vis-à-vis the need for single-minded application to his work. In the words of one of his biographers, Una Pope-Hennessy:

Charles had spirits enough for two, but it was uphill work making this lethargic, unimaginative girl understand just how hard he was working and how anxious he was to make their future secure. "You know that my composition is peculiar . . . and that I can never write till I have got my steam up or . . . until I have become so excited with my subject that I cannot leave off." His "dearest Mouse" and "dearest Life" is exacting and seems incapable of understanding the claims of his profession. One night he writes that he must stay at home, he has not produced sufficient copy to justify him in going out. "If the representations I have so often made to you, be not sufficient to keep you in good humour . . . why then my dear you must be out of humour, and there is no help for it." *

But the lethargy and lack of imagination had its compensations, of course, allowing Dickens for many years to ride roughshod over his wife's personal wishes and inclinations whenever the demands of his job made this necessary or—for he was only human—simply whenever it suited him. In this he was supported by her sister Georgina, one of those devoted dedicated women often found in the background of a superpro's life, arranging, fixing, and protecting him from distractions even within his own family circle.

GREAT MEN AND THE LITTLE WOMAN

Better, though, a weak, colorless, submissive wife than one with a strong personality and conflicting interests. Sometimes people will refer to a star as having "outgrown his wife"—the girl he married in his unknown early years—and wonder at his loyalty or stupidity in keeping her around. What they fail to take into account is the fact that in cases where the little Mouse *is* discarded, the glittering usurper rarely lasts long, precisely because of the ensuing conflict of interests and the consequent distractions to the man's pursuit of his career. And better, too, is the wife who, though not weak and submissive, is sufficiently materialistic, even mercenary, to appreciate the loot the Great Man is capable of bringing home without her being at all interested in how he gets it, and who at the same time is shrewd enough not to do anything to foul up the source. Such a woman the great engineer Isambard Brunel found in Mary Horsley—and "found" here is the

* Una Pope-Hennessy, *Charles Dickens.*

operative word, since the young genius had a pretty canny idea of the sort of person he was looking for in a wife. It was an idea from which was excluded any career-queering propensities. Here he is as a young bachelor of twenty-one, weighing up in his secret journal the very notion of marriage:

Shall I make a good husband?—Am doubtful—my ambition, or whatever it may be called (it is not the mere wish to be rich) is rather extensive. . . .

After all I shall most likely remain a bachelor and that is I think best for me. My profession is after all my only fit wife. . . .

As long as health continues, one's prospects tolerable, and present efforts, whatever they may be, tolerably successful, then indeed a bachelor's life is luxurious: fond as I am of society, *"selfish comfort"* is delightful. I have always felt so. My *châteaux d'Espagne* have mostly been founded on this feeling, what independence! For one whose ambition is to distinguish himself in the eyes of the public, such freedom is almost indispensable—but, on the other hand, in sickness or disappointment, how delightful to have a companion whose sympathy one is sure of possessing! *

In other words, Wedicare.

Of Brunel's subsequent marriage to Mary Horsley, L. T. C. Rolt writes: "It was to prove a tranquil partnership undisturbed, it would seem, by any storms of conflicting temperament." For Mary was a beauty of the hard-core type. She could be obstinate and self-willed over matters of taste and domestic protocol, but in the words of Rolt was "too unemotional and far too level-headed to cross passionate swords with her husband." So long as Brunel lavished money on her for clothes and jewels and on furnishing their home to her standards she was content, while for his part he was happy

* This and subsequent quotations concerning Brunel taken from *Isambard Kingdom Brunel* by L. T. C. Rolt.

to regard her in such clothes and settings as a beautiful "intimately personal symbol of a success in which she played no part." Fortunately for the marriage, his successes were such that Mary never went short of the necessary money. Fortunately, too, Brunel's profession was such that he was rarely at home, being too busy supervising the building of a railroad here, a bridge there, a steamship elsewhere. Her domestic reign, in which she reveled, was never seriously challenged.

Some individuals of incipient genius sidestep the issue altogether by choosing not to marry or even become sexually involved at all. This choice is rarely made in full consciousness—rather do they tend to allow other circumstances or character traits to do the choosing for them, as by giving free full rein to puritanical tendencies, or by the intensive cultivation of a fundamental shyness, or by the nursing of some other psychic wound. Freud was convinced that Leonardo was of this kind, basing the belief on various passages in the great artist's notebooks, like: "Whoso curbs not lustful desires puts himself on a level with the beasts. You can have neither a greater nor a less dominion than that over yourself. It is easier to resist at the beginning than at the end." And so Leonardo began his resistance in adolescence, harnessing his sexual energies for use in his artistic and intellectually creative work—and becoming sexually impotent in the process.

Whatever it was called, *The Love Life of the Superpro* or *Sex and the Single Mind,* it would make a lengthy and fascinating study in itself. But the main objective—whether one sublimates sex or gratifies it, and whether one gratifies it privately or promiscuously—is to get it the hell out of the way of one's work. Long-drawn-out secret affairs are poison. They consume far too much time and, in the need for stratagems, lies, excuses to sustain them, far too much intellectual creative energy. Dickens realized this when he became infatuated with Ellen Ternan and, even in the Victorian England of which he was such a pillar, he went on to cut the corners by kicking his wife out and setting up an establishment for the loved one quite blatantly nearby. It was a big risk. Those of his public who got to know about it were duly shocked. But it was a risk that had to be taken if too great an inroad wasn't to be made on his already overtaxed powers of concentration; and he took it, albeit with a certain amount of near-hysterical bluster. Mercifully, he continued to have the allegiance and active tactical support, even in this venture, of the dedicated Georgina.

Nowadays such matters are handled more coolly, with a quick divorce rather than a somewhat messy separation, or with no divorce at all, the marriage partner treating, or pretending to treat, each sexual side trip as a minor break for refreshment or repair. Such a setup, seemingly carrying matters to fictional extremes, was described long ago by Georges Simenon in *Maigret's Mistake*. Here it is a brilliant surgeon, Professor Gouin, who gets the favored treatment. "People in general have a curious attitude toward geniuses," says his wife. "They are quite prepared to admit that they are different from others where intelligence and professional activity are concerned. . . . Yet these same patients would be shocked to learn that in other ways, too, he is different from them." Maigret, we are told, "could guess what was to follow," and so can we. "The energy he uses up is unbelievable. And the only way in which he has ever been able to relax is with women." Hence the setting up of a girl in a love nest in his own apartment building, hence the hopping into the spare hospital night-shift bed with the nearest available nurse after a particularly tricky stint at the operating table. What few readers *could* guess was also to follow, after an interval of some twenty years, was Simenon's confession in a television interview that, far from being a purely fictional situation, this was in fact his own approach to the problem. The admission was made with equal, almost offhand, and really quite admirable coolness. First came the usual sort of discussion about his powers of concentration, which have to be truly prodigious for anyone to turn out work even of moderate quality at the rate he does. But then it transpired that his sexual appetite was similarly prodigious. And that just as he has found it necessary to have a doctor check him over before the start of every novel, to make sure he can stand the pace, ten or eleven days later, when he's finished it, he finds it necessary to have at least one session with a girl, preferably one who knows her business. And Mme Simenon? Oh, she understands him and his exceptional needs. Why, she sometimes even helps him to select the agent of this unusual therapy. Collapse (almost) of stout interviewer, and no doubt there was many a sympathetic growl among the audience when it further transpired that Mme Simenon was currently in a sanatorium. (Maybe some of them recalled that the understanding Madame Gouin ended in custody, charged with the murder of the love-nest girl.) Yet really, *in the context,* why not? Art is long and the act of relieving the pressure is so very short.

One likes to think that this was what was at the back of the mind of the refreshingly candid movie star Ava Gardner when, in an episode reported by Sheilah Graham, she concluded a hitherto low-key, demure interview with a British lady journalist (during which she had talked in the usual cliché terms about how she wasn't interested in any particular man at the moment, etc., etc.) with these words: "Don't get me wrong, honey, I think fucking is a great sport. It's all the fucking talk you have to listen to from the man before."*

* Quoted from *Scratch an Actor* by Sheilah Graham.

§ 35 §

THE WIFE WITHOUT WHOM...

Besides those individuals who, in the interests of devotion to duty, manage to cope with family ties and those who avoid them altogether, there are some who find themselves in the happy position of having such ties transformed into supports —turned in fact to good positive professional account. This usually occurs when the marriage partner possesses a high degree of managerial skill, yet is willing to lavish it exclusively on the other. Sometimes, as well as the managerial ability, the partner can weigh in as trainer, coach, even collaborator—and so long as he or she is also diplomat enough to perform these functions unobtrusively, all goes well. Such a marriage partner Danny Kaye found in Sylvia Fine—at least in the important early years of his career. During this period, Sylvia busied herself as the comedian's accompanist, the writer of some of his best songs, his rehearsal supervisor, and business manager, performing all these duties so well that his act was molded into the top-quality class that was to earn him stardom in New York and the chance to make it in Hollywood. When this chance came, she continued her efforts, taking care of all the business details as well as managing the household and dealing with all the tedious travel arrangements involved in their regular commuting between Hollywood and New York. In short, it was she who picked up the tabs and the bruises, leaving her husband comparatively free to make the most of his new opportunities. As Kurt Singer sums it up: ". . . he was her creation. His successes had been random and accidental before she created for his special abilities and directed his talents."*

Another strong but devoted partner was Isabel, wife of the great Victorian explorer and translator, Richard Burton. In her, the devotion was compounded of a powerful, at times

* From *The Danny Kaye Saga* by Kurt Singer.

almost hysterical sense of destiny which was modified only by a mysticism that made her willing to triumph vicariously. So she could write, in another premarriage journal:

I worship ambition. . . . By ambition I mean men who have the will and power to change the face of things. I wish I were a man: if I were, I would be Richard Burton. But as I am a woman, I would be Richard Burton's wife. I love him purely, passionately, and devotedly: there is no void in my heart: it is at rest for ever with him.*

This devotion was to be extremely valuable to Burton in times of difficulty and setback, for he was a proud man and suffered deeply on these occasions. The role of The Wife as Soothing Lotion can never have been more efficiently handled than by Lady Burton.

But from the outset she was determined to give more than moral support. Gently nurtured though she was, she learned to cook and do other domestic chores, to look after farmyard animals, to ride, even to fence, in the hope that these accomplishments would be of use to him in the field. (The fencing, she said, would help her "to defend Richard, when he and I are attacked in the wilderness together.") She extended these activities to the intellectual sphere, learning to copy and proofread his manuscripts and—inevitably in such relationships, it seems—to handle his business affairs. And all for him, her hero. Her only purely selfish ambition was to save his soul, she being a devout Catholic and he an atheist.

Burton must have noticed all this with mixed feelings at first. When, after the first seven months of the marriage, he took up a consulship at Fernando Po, he refused to allow her to accompany him even part of the way, and he remained there for eighteen months! On his next longish excursion,

---

* From *The Devil Drives* by Fawn M. Brodie.

however—more of a two- or three-months' retreat from society than a serious expedition—he took her with him and
came to realize it was possible to shape her into a fittingly
tough companion, at the same time appreciating the useful-
ness of some of the practical accomplishments she had trained
for so assiduously earlier.

From then on, his enjoinder to her to "pay, pack, and
follow" reechoes through the partnership like a motto. And
because he was a serious professional traveler, he must have
found her ability to take care of such details much more than
a merely pleasant convenience. In the circumstances, they
could have been nothing short of enormously liberating.
What is more, since Richard's superprofessionalism was primarily of the spirit rather than in terms of remuneration,
Isabel was able to prove herself useful in begging for favors
among influential friends, especially in the matter of securing
suitable and lucrative consulships as springboards for his further questing. A man so intensely proud would never have
been able to bring himself to ask for such favors personally.

So Isabel served the man she idolized, realizing most of
her ambitions through him and being quite content to subject her own very powerful personality to his while he lived.
Only after his death did she override him and pursue that
purely selfish ambition mentioned earlier: by bowdlerizing
or even destroying some of his saltier translations from the
Arabic (she burned *The Scented Garden*) and by doctoring
the record of his last-ditch "conversion."

But for every Sylvia Kaye or Lady Burton, there must be
hundreds of retiring, less gifted marriage partners who are
nonetheless useful to their superpro spouses. Custodians of
privacy; underground fighters for the Great One's freedom
from the anxieties and irritations of day-to-day living; bill
payers; phone answerers; letter writers; mind-guards (to use
Bob Dylan's expression for members of his entourage) as

well as bodyguards; Shielders of the Single Mind. Who was that lady I saw you with last night? That was no lady, that was my bug repellent. Most of them have in fact been wives, though with the emergence of a strong Women's Liberation movement there will no doubt be an increasing number of husbands in the ranks. And sometimes, of course, it is another relative who performs the service—maybe a sister-in-law, as in the Dickens household. Or, as in Wordsworth's, a sister.

A SISTER TO ASSIST HIM

William Wordsworth was an almost classic example of single-mindedness linked with shrewdness and good fortune, and it is worth quoting at some length the opinions of Thomas De Quincey on the subject:

I do not conceive that Wordsworth could have been an amiable boy; he was austere and unsocial, I have reason to think, in his habits; not generous; and, above all, not self-denying. Throughout his later life, with all the benefits of a French discipline in the lesser charities of social intercourse, he has always exhibited a marked impatience of those particular courtesies of life. Not but he was kind and obliging where his services would cost him no exertion; but I am pretty certain that no consideration would ever have induced Wordsworth to burthen himself with a lady's reticule, parasol, shawl. . . . Mighty must be the danger which would induce him to lead her horse by the bridle. Nor would he, without some demur, stop to offer her his hand over a stile. Freedom—unlimited, careless, insolent freedom—unoccupied possession of his own arms, absolute control over his own legs and motions—these have always been so essential to his comfort, that in any case where they were likely to become questionable, he would have declined to make one of the party.*

* This and subsequent quotations regarding Wordsworth are from *Recollections of the Lakes and the Lake Poets* by Thomas De Quincey.

Moreover, the great poet showed a similar solicitude for the freedom of his mind, not only from clutter but also from the encroachment of ideas likely to disturb its habitual tracks (as with Cézanne and some of the others we have touched upon). De Quincey, whose mind was cast in a very different mold, found it hard to understand this, marveling that "very few books sufficed him; he was careless habitually of all the current literature, or indeed of any literature that could not be considered as enshrining the very ideal, capital, and elementary grandeur of the human intellect." To De Quincey it seemed that Wordsworth "in this extreme limitation of his literary sensibilties . . . was as much assisted by that accident of his own intellectual condition, which the Germans of our days have so usefully brought forward to the consciousness, and by which so many anomalies of opinion are solved—viz., his extreme, intense, unparalleled *one-sidedness (einseitigkeit),* as by any peculiar sanity of feeling." And later De Quincey was to strengthen this opinion, giving it the force of a proclamation: "Wordsworth, beyond all men, perhaps, that have ever lived (and very likely as one condition towards the possibility of his own exceeding originality), was *einseitig* in extremity."

There was also the question of luck—a sore topic with the hard-pressed, continually insolvent De Quincey, who wrote that Wordsworth "has not been neglected by fortune; that he has never had the finer edge of his sensibilities dulled by the sad anxieties, the degrading fears, the miserable dependencies of debt; that he has been blessed with competency even when poorest. . . ." And, it could have been added, blessed also with simple tastes and a shrewdness to keep them that way. For it was not all luck and the accident of personality. Before the legacies and the sinecure (the Stamp-Distributorship for the county of Westmoreland),

Wordsworth had the good sense to leave such windfalls out of any reckoning. As De Quincey noted, earlier,

at starting on his career of life, certainly no man had plainer reasons for anticipating the worst evils that have ever persecuted poets, excepting only two reasons which might warrant him in hoping better; and these two were—his great prudence, and the temperance of his daily life. He could not be betrayed into foolish engagements; he could not be betrayed into expensive habits.

But Wordsworth also had the larger shrewdness, the great long-term strategic sense of knowing how to cut the coat of his life according to the cloth of his talent. Here is how De Quincey describes it in operation during the poet's student days:

The advantages of a large college are considerable, both to an idle man who wishes to lurk unnoticed in the crowd, and to the brilliant man, whose vanity could not be gratified by pre-eminence amongst a few. Wordsworth, though not idle as regarded his own pursuits, was so as regarded the pursuits of the place. With respect to them he felt—to use his own words—that his hour was not come; and that his doom for the present was a happy obscurity, which left him, unvexed by the torments of competition, to the genial enjoyment of his life in its most genial hours.

Nevertheless, a poet of Wordsworth's caliber, unknown to the public for much of his professional life, who chooses to live simply, in comparative isolation, even though these conditions admirably suit his natural and professional inclinations, still needs a ready source of constructive appreciation and encouragement. This he found in his sister Dorothy, rather than in his wife: a simple, shy, passive, not particularly clever woman. Dorothy, on the other hand, was lively, intelligent, sensitive, and, above all, devoted—devoted enough to dedicate her life to the great man (rejecting several suitors in order to remain at his side) and deliberately to circumscribe the range of her intellectual interests and pursuits the better to put these at the service of her brother. De Quincey summed up her life as a mission

> to wait upon him as the tenderest and most faithful of domestics; to love him as a sister; to sympathize with him as a confidante; to counsel him as one gifted with a power of judging that stretched as far as his own for producing; to cheer him and sustain him by the natural expression of her feelings—so quick, so ardent, so unaffected—upon the probable effect of whatever thoughts, plans, images he might conceive; finally, and above all other ministrations, to ingraft, by her sexual sense of beauty, upon his masculine austerity that delicacy and those graces which else . . . it would not have had.

A SELF-INDULGING ORDINANCE?

Single-mindedness, as we have seen, can be of incalculable value to the superpro, whether it be a natural gift or a hard-won prize or a hated imposition. (In this last category must come the temporary spartan element that most championship-class boxers have to endure when literally taking to the hills or the forests to train for a big fight in a camp from which wives and girl friends are normally excluded.) Unmitigated, the quality can make a social outcast of an individual, an emotional cripple, a moral monster, a family ogre —and it does seem that very few, if any, can achieve it without incurring such penalties to a greater or lesser degree unless they have close personal assistance of an order that is in itself little short of superprofessional. How is it then that the superpro supporter of the superpro doesn't also become psychologically maimed? The answer, I suppose, is that in fact he, or more usually she, does, but that this never becomes so spectacularly apparent as in the partner who is more fully in the public eye. Furthermore, the contours of the single-minded supporter are softened somewhat by the fact that she is dedicating herself to, or sacrificing herself for, another individual, whereas he is working toward his own glory—the selfish bastard. Should it be offered in his defense that he too is dedicating himself to, or sacrificing himself for, not just an individual but mankind in general, or the enjoyment of countless millions, or any similar concept,* then he'd better leave it for someone else to say it of him, otherwise he'll be castigated as a selfish *and sanctimonious* bastard. And even if someone else does put forward this defense, the subject had better be a poet or a novelist or artist, or someone else with tangible cultural or social legacies—and preferably he should be long dead. What is more, the budding superpro or even the established superpro has to shrug off any sense of injustice or shame, otherwise that state of single-mindedness will most assuredly start to crumble and the standard of his performance will correspondingly suffer.

But having achieved this condition, whether by the hook of heredity or the crook of calculation, and sustained it in spite of all discomforts and distractions, what of the other qualities the superpro must try to cultivate?

---

* Schweitzer himself has come under attack in connection with his family life, such are the penalties of single-mindedness, and of course even Christ is suspect in some quarters because of his brusqueness toward his mother, that day in the temple.

3
Making
the
Best of It

~~~

At one time he would have been called a pacemaker: a good hack specialist making the running for the benefit of a real star; a middle-distance runner, usually, capable of getting out ahead in the first half of a long-distance race and upsetting the timing of the real star's competitors, yet never having any hope of keeping up that pace. Nowadays, in the journalistic haste to build up as a superstar any moderately proficient performer with a colorful personality, they tend to describe him as a "front-runner." In his own right, that is. Without any real star to do his front running for. Such a one ap-

§ 45 §

peared in the 1972 Olympics. "X is a front-runner," the television commentator explained, as the subject leapt into the lead in the first lap. "He must keep that lead because he is a poor finisher."

Well of course X didn't keep that lead. A journalistically built-up star in his own country, he was completely outclassed by the international champions he came up against on that occasion. They used him for what he was. They fed on him. They let him lead for three-quarters of the distance. And then they murdered him.

Had our front-runner really had it in him, he would have done something about that "poor-finisher" record. Just as other overboosted mediocrities in other sports would do something about their well-known deficiencies if they were the superstars they are cracked up to be: the "brilliant" soccer star who can't kick with his left foot, the "great" batter (baseball or cricket) who yet can't handle a certain type of ball. For these are matters of skill, not natural endowment. A man may be too tall or too short or too heavy or too skinny to excel easily or at all, but when it comes to a matter of trainable proficiency there is no excuse for the individual and no possible justification for the accolade of "superstar" or even "star." A real superpro does something about it. Always.

We have to be careful here, though. Sometimes the weakness or deficiency will be the automatic and inevitable result of concentration on a certain asset, and will be accepted by the superpro after considering the overall effect of this displacement of forces and in the light of the general success of the resultant balance. Take that well-known figure in boxing circles, the "fighter without a punch." Usually this means someone without the physique or the technique to deliver a knockout blow. If he has the physique but lacks the technique then he cannot possibly be classed in the top bracket, no matter what his manager or his mother or the sports editor of his hometown paper says. No matter, indeed, how much he might happen to stand out nationally or continentally from a poor crop of competitors. But suppose that deficiency arises as a result of strengthening another aspect of technique, as in Muhammad Ali's case. The physique is there, the dedication and the powers of application and the intelligence to work on the problem. But from the start of his career, Ali was determined to concentrate on speed, agility, and the evasiveness that could be facilitated by his unusually long reach. This inevitably meant a substantial modification of the normal textbook big-hitting technique—the putting of one's whole body into the blow via the shoulder, which involves a massive forward movement, which in turn means putting one's chin well within range of a proficient counterpuncher and thus sacrificing, if only temporarily, any advantage of reach. How then has Ali managed to win so many of his fights by knockouts? By sidestepping the textbooks and perfecting a hitting technique that doesn't depend on body weight: putting into his punches a snap deriving from the arm muscles, assembling combinations of such punches with phenomenal (and well-practiced) speed and accuracy, and making use of the psychological factor so brilliantly described by another world champion, José Torres:

Clay then, and Ali now, has the ability to let punches go with extreme quickness, but most important, at the right moment, just before the man in front of him is able to put his boxer's sense of anticipation to work.

When that happens, the man getting hit doesn't see the punch. As a result, this man's brain can't prepare him to receive the impact of the blow. The eyes couldn't send the message back to the part of the body which would take the shock. So we arrive at one knockout of a conclusion: the punch that puts you to sleep is not so much the hard punch as the punch that you don't see coming.*

In other words, Ali has maximized his chief assets to the extent that they do more than compensate for any natural limitation. They even take care of the limitations arising from the maximizing process itself. And that is professionalism at its very highest level.

But before going on to examine further specific examples it would be useful to take a look at this question (of making the best of one's gifts, of realizing one's full potential, of handling one's deficiencies) in some of its more general aspects.

For instance, is talent or skill *ever* really fully developed? There are of course numerous cases of lazy geniuses who have the ability (as demonstrated if only fitfully—we are not talking about mouth-geniuses now, the if-I-just-had-the-time merchants, who are legion) but lack the application necessary for consistency. And there are even more cases of unlucky geniuses—men and women of great promise whose lives became too complicated through no fault of their own, or whose careers were interrupted or ended by circumstances (international, or natural) completely out of their control, or who —being in professions requiring shrewd management— found themselves brought along too quickly, or held back too late, or victims of vendettas not of their own making. Yet even of those who reach the top and stay there long enough to rate real stardom, it is doubtful if it can ever be said that they are using their talents to the limit. In so many fields so much depends on the competition around—or the standards set—at the time. (Hence the interminable, inevitably inconclusive historical-fictional contests between Ali and Dempsey, say, or Spitz and Weissmuller, and so on, and on. . . .) Then

* This and subsequent Torres quotations are from *Sting Like a Bee*.

again there is the evidence elicited from artificial barriers of the four-minute-mile variety (or the indestructibility of the atom, if it comes to that), which are only valid in the light of known proven techniques: until, in fact, someone comes along with a revolutionary technique that helps him break the barrier, after which hundreds of others begin to pour through and the whole barrier-erecting rigmarole begins again.

What we can be sure of, however, is that most people don't come anywhere near to giving 100 percent of their potential, and that the very fact of neglect produces its own problems, and that it does so on all levels. For just as a boxer operating at only 40 percent capacity (for whatever reason) feels this and, feeling it, lacks the confidence on which certain physical factors depend (like timing and coordination), consequently going on to lose the fight to an inferior opponent working at 70 or 80 percent of *his* capacity, so the ordinary manual worker or executive suffers from the same vicious descending spiral. In the words of Robert Townsend:

All you have to do is look around you to see that modern organizations are only getting people to use about 20 per cent—the lower fifth—of their capacities. And the painful part is that God didn't design the human animal to function at 20 per cent. At that pace it develops enough malfunctions to cause a permanent shortage of psychoanalysts and hospital beds.*

WHEN HUMILITY SCORES DOUBLE

At the basis of the budding superpro's approach to this problem of potential is the factor of appraisal. Usually this means self-appraisal, and even where the individual has, by virtue of the nature of his profession, a sharp-eyed coach or sharp-

* From *Up the Organization.*

eared teacher to do the bulk of the appraising, it is of little value if the pupil is too unintelligent or too arrogant to recognize faults that are pointed out to him.

Now a precondition of self-appraisal is what is usually called humility. It is a misleading term in this context. One's reaction on hearing some notorious prima donna referring to her (or his) "humility" is often one of slight nausea. How hypocritical can these people get?! But in one particular sense it is justified. It has to be if the subject has advanced enough professionally to excel, because excellence simply cannot be achieved without it. In such cases it doesn't mean *modest* or *devoid of vanity* or even *grateful to God* (for bestowing on poor little me the original gift): it simply means that *the subject is always willing to learn something new that might help to improve his performance.* Thus, even at the height of personal success a superstar will always be interested in the performance of a rival, old or up-and-coming. He may go along to sneer, or, if their profession is such that it might eventually bring them into direct combat, to sniff out weaknesses. But if he sees something new that is good, he will be prepared to recognize it (if only silently) and if possible or advisable after due consideration to incorporate the new twist into his own armory.

What goes for the established superpro certainly goes for the aspiring one, no matter how vain or iconoclastic, if he really has what it takes. In order to improve, one must know one's shortcomings. Then one can investigate those shortcomings as they appeared in others who have since eradicated them, in one's heroes and models, or as they still appear in those one despises for being overpraised. And in order to make such investigations and analyses valuable one must learn as much as possible about the chosen field generally. In many cases this is not a conscious process, of course. If one is obsessed with the possibilities of developing a particular skill, one will naturally be interested in every scrap of information on the subject that comes one's way. One "lives, eats, drinks, and sleeps" it, in the old hackneyed phrase. Often the interest is quite indiscriminate. The young aspirant will pick up and thumb through a record book he knows already by heart, in much the same way as nonaspirants will half-consciously riffle through a magazine or newspaper that happens to be at hand, even though they have no interest in its contents. But, conscious or not, selector or absorber, the embryonic superpro is always avid to learn—though in order to *improve,* not merely to make the ranks of the regular professionals; eventually to *excel,* not merely to learn a trade.

Thus when the young Brunel was commissioned to construct a new dock in Sunderland, he made the arduous stagecoach journey from London work for him in many other ways. As his biographer describes it:

When he was on his travels he never missed an opportunity of visiting any work of architectural or engineering interest which might lie on or near his route. Thus he spent some time examining Durham Cathedral when he drove over there in a chaise . . . to deposit the Dock plans and . . . he visited the Scotswood suspension bridge over the Tyne and made a number of detailed sketches. When he finally left Newcastle . . . he embarked upon a regular sightseeing tour, albeit a very purposeful one. His first objective was Stockton where he walked out to inspect the first suspension bridge in England which carried the Stockton and Darlington railway over the Tees. With this he was not impressed. His diary features an alarming sketch showing the floor of the bridge deflected 12 in. by the weight of two coal waggons and the comment: "Wretched thing . . . the floor creaks most woefully in returning." His judgment was correct. . . .

From there he went to Darlington (pausing to survey the town from the church tower) and on, without pausing for sleep, to Hull, where he inspected the docks on arrival, taking dimensions of the entrance locks. Two days later he was traveling on the Manchester-Liverpool railway, timing the journey (probably his first by rail) and making notes.

Interleaved in the diary . . . is a small sheet of paper bearing a series of wavering circles and lines and the inscription: "Drawn on the L & M railway 5.12.31." On this Brunel has added the following significant note: "I record this specimen of the shaking on the Manchester railway. The time is not far off when we shall be able to take our coffee and write while going noiselessly and smoothly at 45 miles per hour—let me try."

And try he was to, later, on the Pullman car of his ambitions —and successfully. But meanwhile, still on the same journey, the process of learning and probing and notetaking and absorbing went on. After breakfasting in Liverpool he visited the docks and the new Custom House (criticizing it harshly) and thence, before the morning was through, to Chester, to inspect the newly completed bridge there.

Similar examples could easily be culled from the early careers of practically anyone who subsequently achieved the heights in his or her chosen profession, though few perhaps show quite the same remarkable energy as this young Victorian dynamo. But Brunel had the advantage of being free from normal career worries. His position, as son of a famous and successful engineer, was assured. There were no doubts about his ever establishing himself simply as a professional. He was free to concentrate on becoming a superpro, with his energies unbled by nagging persistent economic anxieties. Danny Kaye, on the other hand, had still not attained any permanence in his profession, let alone eminence, when he visited China and Japan in 1934 with a small-time comedy-dancing act called the "Terpsichoreans."

The going was tough. The manager of the road show

wasn't impressed by him; there were difficulties with labor agitators and the authorities in Japan; and there was always the language barrier. But (to quote Kurt Singer again):

For all the unpleasantness and difficulties, Danny fell in love with the Orient. Japan and China taught him more than he had hoped for, and the ancient arts and cultures of the countries were both his drama school and university training. He studied the Oriental masters.

The usual popular biography overstatement? Well, maybe— until we get down to details:

In every figurine he absorbed its facial expression, analysed the porcelain figures walking against the wind, coolies bent under heavy loads and the stance of the pompous Mandarin.

Moreover, there was an *immediate* practical necessity to spur him in his studies:

He stayed away from the social gatherings of the troupe, preferring to investigate the alleys and narrow streets, the tiny shops and the unusual foods. He wanted to know the Oriental as a human being so that he could reach their minds and hearts when he was on the stage. He watched carefully to see what gestures made the shop-keeper smile and what tomfoolery evoked laughter from the children in the streets.

Then back to the *general:*

He began to sense that humor is universal, that people the world over smile and laugh at the same things, that a funny face could make a Japanese boy giggle just as it had years ago amused the older boys in the play-yard back at P.S. 149.

On the job itself he was learning all the time as well. To get over the language barrier he experimented with pantomime, making faces and using the finger movements he had carefully studied in Siam to reinforce his expressions. And when he did use his voice it was mainly to pour out torrents of scat-singing gibberish.

Thus, pressed by circumstances and reinforced by his studies, Kaye began maximizing three of his greatest natural assets: his mobile face, his expressive hands, and his nimble tongue.

CONFLICTING INTERESTS

Not all natural assets have a direct contribution to make to their owner's professional skill, however. Sometimes they need diverting into the right channels, and sometimes they have to be suppressed if they are not to be damagingly distracting. In either event, it is a question of control rather than cultivation. Charles Dickens, for example, had a talent for acting that might well have crowded out his writing talent, had it not been for a bout of toothache. As a young man, he became seriously involved in cultivating the former talent, spending his spare evenings at the theatre, studying the impersonations of Charles Mathews, memorizing parts, taking acting lessons from a professional, and practicing assiduously in front of a mirror. Then, when he considered himself ready, he applied for and was granted an audition at Covent Garden—an appointment he had to cancel because of a swollen face. Before he could make another he was overtaken by success as a political journalist—a success of such force that it swept the theatrical aspirations beyond the bounds of practicability.

Were the two talents of equal strength in this case? It is not unlikely, when we consider the tremendous success of Dickens's dramatic readings later in his life. But, fortunately for posterity, the taste of success provided its usual alchemy, turning general hope into an intensely burning ambition.

Indeed, who is to say that this wasn't fortunate for his contemporaries too, cheated out of a potentially great actor though they were? While it is difficult to see how his writing talent could have significantly fed his acting skills, it is certain that the histrionic propensities, duly controlled and assimilated, did much to enrich his writing.

But Dickens was superprofessional enough not to stop there. There is something of the Chicago stockyards about such men and women in that they will instinctively squeeze the last ounce of value out of a natural asset, whether it be a major or contributory one. So in this case the hooves were made into glue, the horns into hatpegs, with the acting flair and experience being used in the *business of being a writer,* as well as in the writing itself. In his early days it helped him to carry himself with assurance in the exalted and influential social circles to which he began to get invited; and even when he was well established as a celebrity, it helped him to look the part on his tours abroad.

He was visiting America in the role of a distinguished author and therefore must provide himself with fashionably-cut coats, coloured vests, and the brocade dressing-gowns in which gentlemen gave interviews to callers before donning their frock-coats for the street. He must also buy for his adornment new tie-pins, chains and rings.

VIRTUES OF NECESSITY

Maximizing one's assets is only one aspect of making the best of oneself, however. A more hazardous and difficult task is the handling of deficiencies, whether by eradicating them altogether, or compensating for them, or in some way harnessing them. The eradication of straightforward technical deficiencies has already been touched on and need not detain us here. When a would-be star (or his coach) notices a persistent flaw in his technique, he either practices hard until he gets rid of it or shrugs it off and remains a would-be. Similarly, if it is a problem of physique that can be solved by treatment—by dieting, say, or even by an operation—the true superpro goes ahead with that treatment without further question. But when the detrimental condition is inoperable —totally ineradicable—the subject has to approach it in terms of compensation and, where possible, amelioration. Nothing, for instance, can be done about shortness of stature once the body is fully grown. Therefore a short aspirant in a sport where tallness is an asset has to do something to make up for this, and make up for it in a big way if his aspirations are toward the top. In tennis, such a person might concentrate on building up his strength, on increasing the sheer power of his shots, like Lew Hoad; or on accuracy and consistency, like Ken Rosewall. Similarly, in a sport where shortness and lightness are assets, as in horse racing, the aspiring star jockey who grows beyond a certain height has to make the necessary adjustments or quit.

Lester Piggott, the British champion jockey, provides us with an excellent example of compensation, plus amelioration, plus the actual transformation of a defect into an asset. At five feet seven and a half, he is far taller than most of his professional colleagues. Even before attaining that height, most riders would probably have given up any ambition to race professionally and settled for some less physically demanding aspect of the business. Piggott's ambition, however, was too burning to allow him to do this, and he resigned himself to a permanent diet that brings his weight down to around twenty pounds lower than it should be for a man of his height. As he has put it himself:

I've got to earn my living in a pretty strenuous game working at about 1½ stone below my natural weight. Some people exaggerate how I live: I don't starve, and I don't live on cigars and the *Financial Times,* and I don't drive to every race meeting in a rubber suit. But you can't eat and drink what might come naturally to you.

If I'm riding at eight stone six [118 pounds], I have a boiled egg and a bit of toast for breakfast. If I have to do eight stone five that day, I'll give up the egg. I have a sandwich in the jockeys' room after I've finished riding, and I'll always have a meal at night. You lose the habit of eating, really . . .*

But having brought his weight down to that level, and kept it there, he finds that height itself can have its compensations —that height divorced from weight can in fact be an asset. Piggott has come to regard this as his main advantage: "If you've got a good length of leg, you can communicate more with the horse, squeeze him with your knees, control him generally—show him you are there." Which more than makes up for the disadvantage in terms of riding style:

Style is how you look. If you're small, it doesn't matter so much how you look, there isn't so much of you to be seen. And your legs don't take up so much room. If you're big, you can be seen better, and there's less horse showing.

It's difficult for me to look stylish because I like to ride short. People ask me why I ride with my bottom in the air. Well, I've got to put it somewhere.

Even at twenty pounds below his natural weight, Piggott is still on the heavy side for a jockey. But then this means he doesn't have to carry so much dead weight—the lead under the saddle—to make up the right scale.

If a jockey is strong, and he's good, I reckon live weight is better than dead weight. If all of the weight the horse is carrying is

* In an interview with Kenneth Harris, the London *Observer,* 7 June 1970.

live, and the jockey can put it in the right place at every stride, the horse runs freer than he would if part of the weight is in a fixed place, in a bag on his back.

Piggott has solved this particular problem by physical self-denial, just as so many superpros—no doubt himself included—have to deny themselves less tangible but no less attractive pleasures, spiritual and psychological, in the interests of maintaining their single-mindedness and freedom from distraction. People with naturally ascetic or masochistic inclinations will obviously find such sacrifices less irksome than their hedonistic fellows—and that might well account for Florence Nightingale's endurance of severe privations in the Crimea. (That and the fact that her profession essentially consisted in the combating of privation.) But even she can hardly have allowed for the curious situation that confronted her on her return to England, when she discovered her new-found fame itself to be a drawback in her campaign for the reform of army conditions, and she had deliberately to discount it and even to smother it.

The situation arose in this way:

On her return from the Crimea, in spite of her great fatigue, she was determined that something must be done quickly to eradicate the causes of the disaster in which 73 percent of the British Army mortality rate, in six months, had been from disease alone. Her clear cool analytical mind had noted precisely where the root of the trouble lay: in the lumbering, buck-passing, badly directed health administration system. Quite obviously the only real solution was the most radical reform of that system. But the question of organizing pressure for such a reform was a thorny one. In particular, she was hampered by two great handicaps, as she confessed in a letter to a friend. The first—that she was a woman in what was still essentially a man's world—she had

had to cope with all along and might be expected to cope with again. But the second—the fact that she was now a popular heroine, and so an even greater force to be resisted by the entrenched bureaucrats—was something entirely new. Combined with the first, it seemed to render completely hopeless her prospects of getting anywhere in her new task.

So here was a woman faced with the seemingly paradoxical fact that fame itself was a weakness in her armory. What should she do? Accept it as inevitable, capitalize on it, and hope that as a weapon it would prove powerful enough? Most people in her position, even those experienced in the ways of coping with resistance to reform, might have taken that line, accepting it as a kind of Hobson's choice that might yet pay off, given *sufficient* popular support. But, thanks to the unshakable intellectual grasp she had on matters that concerned her, Florence Nightingale knew her public inductively as well as she knew her opposition empirically. She declined an official invitation from the authorities to put forward her suggestions for improvements, suspecting, no doubt rightly, that they would be rejected out of hand, and had only been sought so that they could be given this treatment. Then she set about systematically dismantling the public heroine image, discounting the fame whenever she could and stolidly refusing to do anything to sustain it. In the words of one of her biographers:

After Miss Nightingale's return from the Crimea she never made a public appearance, never attended a public function, never issued a public statement. Within a year or two most people assumed she was dead. . . . The authorities expected that on her return she would make revelations. She neither revealed, nor attacked, nor justified herself. She wrote nothing; she made no speeches; she was not even seen. . . . She refused interviews, receptions, presentations. She refused to go out to dine. She refused to be painted. "The publicity and talk there have been about

4

Respecting
Mistakes

"The man who makes no mistakes," said one E. J. Phelps in
a speech at the Mansion House, London, on 24 January 1899,
"does not usually make anything."

Samuel Smiles put it only slightly differently:

"We often discover what *will* do, by finding out what
will not do; and probably he who never made a mistake never
made a discovery."

"Experience," sighed Oscar Wilde through *Lady Win-
dermere's Fan,* "is the name everyone gives to their mistakes."

And there is the old Latin proverb:

"Wise men learn by other men's mistakes; fools, by their own."

Thus, in even so short an anthology, we run the gamut of attitudes toward mistakes, ranging from the slob's excuse (to which the answer might be: "Sure we all make mistakes—but *all* the time?"), through the complacency of the amateur ("The more mistakes I make the more likely am I to hit on something good" is what Messrs. Phelps and Smiles really seem to be saying), to the two kinds of pro reaction. For in the Wilde quotation there is surely more than a breath of the weary wisdom of the regular plodder, who knows the value of analyzing one's mistakes, yet has the guilty knowledge that there *are* other, quicker, brighter ways of learning; while in the Latin tag there is all the harshness and arrogance and protective dishonesty of a certain type of superpro. (To any ordinary mortal it might seem that fools are precisely those who do *not* learn by their mistakes, that perhaps the old Roman should have cited, well, "ordinary mortals." But the point is that to our Mr. Big—or Senator Giganteus—the fools start precisely there, with the ruck. Where the dishonesty comes in—and the swagger cannot cover it entirely—is with the assumption that the superpro never makes a mistake, which is absurd, but which is also a necessary comfort or prop to a certain type of personality, *and harmless enough so long as he qualifies it in private, if only in his heart.*)

Since it is the professional and superprofessional attitudes to mistakes that concern us here, let us return for a moment to the "front-runner with the poor finish" of the previous section. Let us, in fact, assume that this athlete really had a great potential, and that the poor finishing was not a basic ineradicable deficiency, that it was due entirely to some mistake. Naturally, he would be anxious, eagerly anxious, to do something about it. But what? How does an embryonic or established superpro handle his mistakes? What is his approach to the whole subject likely to be?

First, simple and obvious though it may seem, I think there is an overriding need for such an individual (and especially the budding superpro) to *concede* the fact that a mistake has been made and not to brush it off as part of "just one of those days"; or the fault of an unfamiliar diet (once the favorite excuse of English soccer players after defeat on the Continent); or any other of the dozens of excuses that the mediocre (so often more nimble and inventive in this than in their basic art or craft) can always drum up. Then again—in fields where there is no clear-cut losing of a race or contest to make absolutely plain the fact of a flaw or fault or shortcoming (not to call it a mistake)—it is necessary for the would-be star to *recognize* as a flaw, fault, or shortcoming, etc., something that might have brought him a measure of success in a less demanding atmosphere. Here, for example, is how the great theatrical director Stanislavski caught himself in the very act, as it were, when rehearsing a part in one of his early professional appearances as a player, under the direction of his hero, the producer and the actor Fedotov:

And so I began to imitate Fedotov. Of course I copied him only outwardly, for it is impossible to copy the living spark of genius. The trouble was that I, a sworn imitator, was at the same time a very bad imitator. Imitation is a special gift that I did not possess. When my imitation was unsuccessful, I left it and caught hold of my old methods of play, seeking life in the tempo of patter and waving my arms, then in acting without a pause so that the spectator might not have time to be bored, or in the straining of all my muscles and the squeezing out of temperament, or in the loss of text. In a word, I was fatally returning to my former amateur and musical comedy mistakes, which can be covered in one sentence:

"Play as hard as you can while your audience is not asleep."

"They praised me for it before. I was joyful and light and funny on the stage."

But my attempts to commit my former errors were not accepted by Fedotov. He would cry from his place:

"Don't mumble! Clearer! Do you think that this will make me, the spectator, laugh? Just the opposite; you bore me, because I don't understand anything. Your stamping, and waving your arms, and walking, and all your numberless gestures interfere with my vision. There are spots in my eyes and a noise in my ears. Whatever made you think it was funny?" *

Happy indeed is the embryonic superpro who has his Fedotov at hand to show him the error of what he'd imagined to be such winning ways.

Together with a readiness to concede that a mistake might have been made (whether discovered for oneself or pointed out by others) there should also be, in the superstar's mental equipment, an ever-ready pinch of salt to apply to that possibility. By this I mean a question in some such terms as the following: *Allowing that something has not gone according to plan, is it in fact 100 percent a mistake, or might it not be one of those deviations, those untoward happenings, those freaks, that from time to time point to a new discovery, or to some revolutionary technique that raises standards to heights not hitherto considered possible?* As with Kepler, whose pinch turned out to be more of opium than salt, in this instance described by Arthur Koestler:

. . . he *knew* that his inverse-ratio "law" (between a planet's speed and solar distance) was incorrect. . . . But, he argues, the deviation is so small that it can be neglected. Now this is true for Earth, with its small eccentricity, yet not at all true for Mars, with its large eccentricity. Yet even toward the end of the book

* This and the following Stanislavski quotations are from his *My Life in Art.*

. . . long after he had found the correct law, Kepler speaks of the inverse-ratio postulate as if it were true not only for Earth, but also for Mars. He could not deny, even to himself, that the hypothesis was incorrect; he could only forget it. Which he promptly did. Why? Because, though he knew that the postulate was bad geometry, it made good physics to him, and therefore ought to be true. The problem of the planetary orbits had been hopelessly bogged down in its purely geometrical frame of reference, and when Kepler realized that he could not get it unstuck, he tore it out of that frame and removed it into the field of physics. This operation of removing a problem from its traditional context and placing it into a new one, looking at it through glasses of a different color, as it were, has always seemed to me of the very essence of the creative process.

MISTAKE . . . OR WORSE?

The ability to concede and recognize one's mistakes is something that every superpro has to cultivate from the outset of his career. Later, and particularly during the middle—one might almost say the menopausal—stages of such a career, however, a new demand is sometimes made on the star's perceptivity: a requirement that in the face of lack of success he be able to *convince* himself of the fact that it is indeed a mistake that has been made and is not a general natural failure of power, a falling off, the final inevitable lapse into obsolescence. A top-class fighter, for example, might at the peak of his career be matched with an unorthodox opponent. To meet this new type of challenge he, or his handlers, might decide on a change of technique. Now there are always several choices open in a situation of this sort, and the more unusual the style of fighting to be dealt with, the fewer the precedents (other men's mistakes, let us say) there are to work upon. So there is a greater chance of making a wrong choice. And so our fighter goes into the ring, having opted for the wrong tactics, and gets badly beaten. An honorable mistake? Of course. And one that accepted and recognized as such can be analyzed and used the next time the situation arises. But too often in cases like this there is no next time, simply because the defeated champion finds it too hard to convince himself that a mistake has been made at all. Pride might have something to do with it, of course—too long a run of success putting beef into too arrogant and too self-convincing a posture of infallibility—the sort of pride that, coming before a fall, can make it such a crippling one. But more usually it is a deeper, darker, more logical factor at work: the specter that comes visiting champions at four o'clock in the morning, whispering, *How much longer, buddy?*—or thoughts to that effect. At such a stage, natural honesty and natural fear combine to make it all too easy to concede total permanent defeat instead of a merely temporary lapse. And that perhaps is why —to paraphrase the proverb books again—champions so rarely come back.

It can happen in most other fields, if not indeed in all. And the mistakes involving the mid-career superpro need not even be his own. They can be made by others, disastrously implicating him. As for instance when faulty production ruins an actor's new movie or series—something on which perhaps he'd set so much hope, as a new point of departure. For that is another thing. The better the pro the more experimental he is likely to be, the more restless, the less likely to be content to repeat himself. It is inevitable, therefore, that the older such an individual grows, the more vulnerable he becomes in this respect.

Writers seem particularly prone to looking on the blackest possible side. One of the best British novelists of the last three or four decades—a cautious experimentalist—gave up writing several years ago because a batch of unfavorable reviews convinced him he was "no longer in touch with modern living." This at the age of about fifty—an age when so many of the greatest interpreters of their times were just getting into their stride. What then should he have done? What would one of our postulated superpros have done? If he'd been convinced of the literal truth of the reviewers' charge, only one thing: gone out and got himself back into touch. If on the other hand, working on half a lifetime's knowledge of the very understandable failings and weaknesses of reviewers, he'd suspected they were right in their condemnation or misgivings but hopelessly off target with their reasons (they have to shoot so hastily and in such cramped positions, after all), he would have looked in that last book for mistakes: plain ordinary lapses, whether of timing or tone, structure or texture. One suspects that Hemingway took just such a course after the critical debacle of *Across the River and into the Trees*—and then came right back with *The Old Man and the Sea.*

Henry James's greatest mistake was strategic rather than tactical. It was perpetrated—and on a monumental scale— over a period of four or five years around the crucial age of fifty, when he embarked on his protracted experiment of writing for the theatre. Of the five original plays he wrote in this period, only one, *Guy Domville,* was produced—and the author was booed off the stage when he went to take his call on the opening night. It survived for thirty-one performances, as it happened, but the signs were clear enough, and at once the natural middle-aged tendency to sink into depression began to operate: "I have felt, for a long time past," he told a friend, "that I have fallen upon evil days—every sign or symbol of one's being in the least wanted, anywhere or by anyone, having so utterly failed. A new generation, that I know not, and mainly prize not, has taken universal possession."

But he didn't allow himself to stay down there for long.

A mere eighteen days after that catastrophic opening, we find him writing in his notebook the famous affirmatory lines:

I take up my *own* old pen again—the pen of all my old unforgettable efforts and sacred struggles. To myself—today—I need say no more. Large and full and high the future still opens. It is now indeed that I may do the work of my life. And I will.

So much whistling in the dark? Indian talk? There is an element of that in it, certainly, and no one could have been more entitled to such an indulgence. But what transforms it entirely, making it the utterance of a really great professional, is the very next sentence—simple, practical, bleak, necessary:

I have only to *face* my problems.

And face them he did, to the extent that he could write, only three weeks later, detailed notes on the themes of what were to become *The Wings of a Dove* and *The Golden Bowl*. At that stage they were intertwined in a single possible project, on which he makes the following observations:

I seem to see it as a nominal 60,000 words: which *may* become 75,000. *Voyons, voyons:* may I not instantly sit down to a little close, clear, full scenario of it? As I ask myself the question, *with* the very asking of it, and the utterance of that word so charged with memories and pains, something seems to open out before me, and at the same time to press upon me with an extraordinary tenderness of embrace. Compensations and solutions seem to stand there with open arms for me—and something of the "meaning" to come to me of past bitterness, of recent bitterness that otherwise has seemed a mere sickening, unflavoured draught. Has a *part* of all this wasted passion and squandered time (of the last 5 years) been simply the precious lesson, taught me in that roundabout and devious, that cruelly expensive, way, *of the singular value for a narrative plan too* of the (I don't know *what* adequately to call it) divine principle of the Scenario?

That "divine principle" was to be of immense use to him in clarifying and tightening the plots of some of his greatest novels.

THE MEASURE OF A MISTAKE

Such then is one of the most important psychological aspects of mistakes as related to the work of a superpro, and it is something to which we shall be returning in later chapters. Meanwhile, it is worth examining in some detail the ways of evaluating individual mistakes once they have been recognized as such, whether grudgingly or with gratitude.

One of the first crop of questions to be asked might well be: Is there a generic factor? Is there some root cause that might give rise to a multiplicity of similar errors, or at least to a disturbing and possibly disastrous recurrence, in the future? For instance, did it arise from a tendency to experiment? And, if so, are the benefits deriving from this tendency sufficiently valuable to offset such mistakes? Should it, in fact, continue to be cultivated? Or should it be scrapped? Or can it be brought under finer control?

Then again, has the root cause something to do with general attitudes? Overconfidence? Loss of confidence? Can the former be curbed without a lapse into the latter? Can the latter be remedied? Or is it a question of false hope—a mixture of overconfidence and wishful thinking—the old, old question? Here is that old, old superpro Machiavelli on the subject:

Speaking to the disparagement of an enemy is usually due to the arrogance aroused in you by victory or by the false hope of victory. False hopes of this kind not only cause men to make mistakes in what they say, but also what they do. For, when such hopes enter men's breasts they cause them to dispense with caution, and often to miss the chance of obtaining a sure thing in the hope, but by no means the certainty, of improving on it.*

Or (to continue the series of exploratory questions) could it be the more insidious, often tortuously and tenaciously rooted variety of causes: the inherited tendency, the possibly fatal flaw that has been taken over with, and obscured by, the benefits derived from a respected model or mentor or predecessor? That possibility too must be investigated and faced up to if found operative—no matter how great the sacrifice or how daunting the resultant reappraisal may threaten to be. Such an error is serious enough when it affects a technique, as Carl Flesch, the great violin teacher, was at pains to point out:

In this connection we often have to struggle against an inner opposition, of which we ourselves are not conscious. The fact is that there are fingerings and bowings which, though we may feel they are illogical or out of date, are closely connected in our recollections with the achievements of some artist enthusiastically adored in youthful days, and from which, during the remainder of our life, reverence prevents us from freeing ourselves. Reasons of this kind often are responsible for the retention of quite notoriously primitive fingerings and bowings, representing some interpreter's individual legacy.†

But naturally this situation is at its most agonizing in fields involving years of patient detailed groundwork, as in scientific research. Kepler—whose work on the motions of the planets was responsible for founding the modern vision of the universe (his first two planetary laws providing the neces-

---

* This and following quotations from Machiavelli are from *The Discourses.*
† From *The Art of Violin Playing,* by Carl Flesch, as are later quotations about violin playing.

sary basis for Newton's gravitational law)—offers a striking example of this in his great work *A New Astronomy*.

The book itself took him six years to write and is a step-by-step, almost blow-by-blow account of the calculations leading to his discoveries, sparing the reader no detail of all the sidetracks and dead ends into which Kepler was led along the route. As has already been mentioned, many of his difficulties arose because, quite naturally, he started out by thinking and working along the geometrical lines of his great predecessors, and it was this that got him into such terrible statistical contortions when pursuing his specific inquiry into the movement of Mars, hitherto irreducible into any known system. Working on four of his predecessor Tycho de Brahe's numerous observations of the positions of the planet, he covered 900 folio pages of draft calculations (in small handwriting) in a trial-and-error effort to make them the basis of a satisfactory hypothesis. No wonder that at times (to quote Koestler's words): "he felt, like Rheticus, that a demon was knocking his head against the ceiling, with the shout, 'These are the motions of Mars!' " But at last Kepler managed to hammer out his hypothesis, describing the event at the end of the relevant chapter with the words:

Thou seest now, diligent reader, that the hypothesis based on this method not only satisfies the four positions on which it was based, but also correctly represents, within two minutes, all the other observations . . .

This was followed by three pages of tables to prove the validity of his claims.

But then he began the next chapter thus:

Who would have thought it possible? This hypothesis, which so closely agrees with the observed oppositions, is nevertheless false. . . .

It had failed to stand up to the test application of two more of Tycho's observations, which threw all the rest out by an unacceptable margin of eight minutes.

Later he writes:

And thus the edifice which we erected on the foundation of Tycho's observations, we have now again destroyed. . . . This was our punishment for having followed some plausible, but in reality false, axioms of the great men in the past.

Ironically, at an earlier, seemingly more successful stage of his researches, he had written about another misguided worker in the field:

Oh, for a supply of tears that I may weep over the pathetic diligence of Apianus who, relying on Ptolemy, wasted his valuable time and ingenuity on the construction of spirals, loops, helixes, vortices, and a whole labyrinth of convolutions, in order to represent that which exists only in the mind, and which Nature entirely refuses to accept as her likeness.

Kepler was of course undaunted—as the somewhat masochistic tone of his commentary indicates—and he went on to account for that eight-minute discrepancy by his revolutionary application of physical rather than geometrical reasoning. In doing this, not only did he lay the foundation of modern astronomy, he also introduced a new professionalism, a superprofessionalism, into the field. And that is at least equally important. As Koestler points out, Kepler's decision to press on regardless

was the final capitulation of an adventurous mind before the "irreducible, obstinate facts." Earlier, if a minor detail did not fit into a major hypothesis, it was cheated away or shrugged away. Now this time-hallowed indulgence had ceased to be permissible. A new era had begun in the history of thought: an era of austerity and rigor.

§ 72 §

But to end this subsection nearer home, let us come to earth with (shall we say?) a bounce—on the fairway of a championship golf course. The spirit of the individuals concerned is the same, and the agony—only the venue and the time have been changed. I am thinking now of an example of the mistake that arises, and tends to recur, through a simple mechanical process of adjustment to some larger trouble —something connected with a natural deficiency—and the far from simple decision that then has to be made: Do something about it, or leave reasonably well alone? Ben Hogan's slashing is the case in point—the problem of a great golfer who had had to make up for his shortness by developing a whipcord motion in striking the ball, together with an unusually long swing, the success of the whole action depending on accurate timing. But, excellent though Hogan's timing was, it was never 100 percent reliable, and there were times when the ball flew off to the left and got him into trouble. Nevertheless he was highly successful and, as Tom Scott and Geoffrey Cousins have pointed out in the book from which this example has been drawn: "it is never easy for a man to change his style when wins are coming at a steady rate."* In fact it was probably only as the result of a serious car accident that almost cost him his life that Hogan did get down to correcting the fault. Finding that he could no longer swing the club so far back and that this made for greater smoothness despite a lessening of power, he was able to make up for the loss of distance by his ability to place the ball—an ability he went on to use to devastating effect.

AMENDMENTS—AND ADAPTATIONS

The correction of mistakes, once recognized and evaluated, is too diverse a topic to deal with in much particularity here,

* *Golf Secrets of the Masters*, by Tom Scott, with Geoffrey Cousins.

beyond observing that with the few exceptions already noted, where a mistake might be considered best ignored, the super-pro will go to every length to get it put right or prevent its recurrence. If the basic fault is obvious, so is the remedy likely to be; and in most cases the individual, drawing on his own experience and knowledge, will be able to devise satisfactory ways of tackling the problem. It is when those remedies are tedious, involving long periods of hard work, that the men are sorted from the boys: the pro tennis player who can't rest until he has practiced and practiced the stroke that he bungled and thereby lost a match, from the happy Larrys who will be content to wash away the rancid flavor of defeat with a few extra drinks and a tomorrow's-another-day philosophy. Similarly, if a remedy is not easy to discover, the superpro will keep on plugging away until he has found it. Pride will go by the board in such a situation—even if it means donning a disguise when visiting a likely coach, even if it means consulting a rival who seems to have conquered the same kind of fault. And if it means hiring spies or brib-ing servants, ethics won't be allowed to stand in the way, either.

But these are dramatic extremes. In cases of such diffi-culty, what usually comes to the rescue again is the obses-sional hunger for facts about their professions that most stars are afflicted with. (Remember, always, the scholarly gardener of Westminster.) Thus, out of the welter of ac-cumulated and secreted information drawn or simply ab-sorbed from the annals of the sport or craft or art or business in question, there will emerge instances of similar mistakes and their corrections. Machiavelli had a word on this, too, albeit in a grander, wider context:

If the present be compared with the remote past, it is easily seen that in all cities and in all peoples there are the same desires

and the same passions as there always were. So that, if one examines with diligence the past, it is easy to foresee the future of
any commonwealth, and to apply those remedies which were
used of old; or, if one does not find that remedies were used, to
devise new ones owing to the similarity between events.

It was only because he was writing in what he considered to
be an era of political slobbishness that he had to add with
some weariness:

But, since such studies are neglected and what is read is not understood, or, if it be understood, is not applied in practice by
those who rule, the consequence is that similar troubles occur
at all times.

Finally, a note on a rather paradoxical aspect of the
subject: the deliberate mistake. In this context, I am not
referring to the simple stratagem contemptuously dismissed
by Machiavelli when he stated that "the general of an army
ought not to rely on an obvious mistake which an enemy is
seen to make, for it will always be a fraud, since it is not
reasonable that men should so lack caution." That is the
deliberately manufactured mistake. But in professions involving combat or contest a notorious weakness can be extremely useful to its victim, if he is able to remedy it secretly.
Then it may be so simulated as to lead even the most cautious and Machiavellian of his opponents into a trap. (Just
once, of course. But in any contest of superpros that once
can be enough.) Or—to return to the phenomenal Ali—the
remedial step might even be left out altogether: the genuine
mistakes and his opponent's awareness of them being used
in the same contest, to the opponent's utter confusion. Thus,
on the 1970 Ali-Quarry fight, José Torres could write:

He still had speed, but he made all those mistakes [arising from
Ali's habit of pulling away]. . . . Yet, once again, he had gotten

away with them. Ali, in fact, had used his mistakes to fool the other guy. I thought I knew why. Ali knows when he's doing wrong. He invites you to take advantage of it. But Ali is two steps ahead. He *knows* what your next two punches are going to be.

So much, then, for mistakes and a superpro's ability to come to terms with them, correct them, learn from them, use them. What it amounts to really is a *respect* for mistakes such as the Romans had (in spite of that old Latin tag). Let Machiavelli explain:

The Romans . . . were not only less ungrateful than other republics; they were also more considerate and more careful in punishing the commanders of [their] armies than was any other republic. For even if they had made a mistake with evil intent, their punishment was still humane; while, if it was due to ignorance, the Romans did not punish, but rewarded and honoured the person concerned. This mode of procedure met with their approval because they held it to be of supreme importance to those who commanded their armies, that in mind they should be free and unembarrassed, and should not have to concern themselves with irrelevant matters in arriving at their decisions, for they did not wish to add fresh difficulties and dangers to what was already a difficult and dangerous task, since, were they thus encumbered, there would be none who would ever act virtuously.

It is a respect echoed in modern times by such a superpro as Robert Townsend, former general of the Avis army cohorts:

Admit your own mistakes openly, maybe even joyfully.

Encourage your associates to do likewise by commiserating with them. Never castigate. Babies learn to walk by falling down. If you beat a baby every time he falls down, he'll never care much for walking.

§ 76 §

My batting average on decisions at Avis was no better than .333. Two out of every three decisions I made were wrong. But my mistakes were discussed openly and most of them corrected with a little help from my friends.*

* From *Up the Organization.*

others applaud it as the rightful flaunting of an emblem of rank. And the application of the term goes far beyond the opera house—to be linked, usually pejoratively, with the behavior of sports stars and celebrities of all kinds, even to the little local luminaries of amateur dramatic societies and village tennis clubs, or beyond that, into the workaday world, to describe displays of pique in the typing pool or bombast in the boardroom. Similar misconceptions riddle the question of "artistic temperament"—as something extraneous to the *real* working of the subject's mind, to the *necessary* applications of force involved in his or her tasks.

Then again there is the half-truth so frequently uttered —not without a dogmatic complacency in many cases—by the antiprima-donnas: that it is necessary for all superpros to exercise firm control over their emotions at all times. And there are some of these critics who then follow up by asserting the quarter-truth: that without such control no individual can be a true superstar. Now this is something that might deserve more respect if the propounders meant by "control" what it usually means: an ability to step up as well as clamp down. But more often than not only the clamping down is meant.

At the root of such misconceptions is the fact that there are many different kinds of professions, making many different kinds of emotional demands on the participators. There are professions where true phlegm is vital to a good performance—most of the time. There are professions where a phlegmatic approach could be ruinous to a good performance—most of the time. And there are professions where the balance has to be more even than in either of those cases.

Thus, most of the time, an operating surgeon must be sure to keep his emotions under anaesthetic, along with the patient. But if he chooses to vent some of his suppressed feelings on an assistant or colleague, either between operations or the phases of one operation, and if by so doing it helps steady him for the main work—fine. Conversely, an actor, most of the time, should be careful to cultivate the free play of his emotions, to keep his responses limber, as it were, tuned up, ready to go, ready in fact to be *finely* controlled, which means *both ways* with delicacy, when actually performing. To make a practice of restraining emotion in such a case could cause severe damage to the necessary mechanism.

Of the professions requiring a fairly balanced mixture of ready feeling—even great sensitivity—and detachment, perhaps imaginative writing is the most obvious. Without such sensitivity of feeling, an author's work would be shallow and lifeless, whereas without the restraint it would be strident or in some other way lacking in its maximum potential effect. Vis-à-vis his emotions, a writer of fiction is, oddly enough, somewhat in the position of the great nonfiction writer Theodore White, when riding on horseback through famine-stricken China: "You must suppress every human instinct you have to stop and help. You spur your horse on because if you stop they slash at it and eat the flesh off." It was to prevent such a flaying on the spiritual plane—a flaying of his own talent—that Dickens delayed writing about the horrors of the Manchester cotton mills that he'd witnessed on trips there in 1838 and 1839. Superprofessional that he was, he knew that his main persuasive strength as a writer lay in sentiment and humor, modes of treatment that had to wait for his immediate anger to become cooler and more manageable.

But to return to the subject of prima-donnaishness itself, we can probably do no better than examine the behavior of a real prima donna in every sense of the word: Maria Callas. A good instance is the one in which she canceled her contract with the New York Met because the manager decided to schedule two performances of Verdi's *Macbeth* between two of *La Traviata.* Her objection was simple and artistically very sane. In the opinion of her mother (then bitterly estranged from her daughter and so without any of the usual maternal bias):

. . . she has never been more right. Violetta la Traviata is a fragile character, whose death is part of her star-crossed love but whose role, so sweet and wistful, should be sung by a lyric soprano or even a coloratura. Lady Macbeth, on the other hand, is more than an ambitious bitch; she is a tragic character who not only drives a man to murder but commits murder herself. Hers is a role which must be sung in the dark and ominous voice of impending doom. The switch from the sweetly pathetic to the forcefully tragic and back again would most likely have produced two poor performances out of four. When she was young, Maria more than once made such trying shifts without much rest between operas, but having reached the top of the operatic ladder she can no longer afford a single slip. She must always be at her best. This may be art for Maria's sake rather than art for art's sake, as she says, but it is opera and opera audiences who benefit in the long run.*

So Callas blew up and blew out, saying such things as her voice was not an elevator to go up and down at the whim of Mr. Metropolitan; and so millions of people around the world shrugged and observed, with a grin or a snort, that Callas was acting like a prima donna again. We may be sure, however, that very few people would observe, with or without a grin or a snort, that Mr. Bing was acting like a theatre manager again, with his perfectly proper eye to the exigencies of the front office and the jealousy of other singers. It may be argued that Callas should have made her protests in a different, quieter, more businesslike way—behaving like a

* From *My Daughter—Maria Callas* by Evangelia Callas and Lawrence G. Blochman.

theatre manager herself, in fact. Yet she was no theatre manager any more than Bing was a great soprano, and for her to
have played the dispute his way would have meant being
hopelessly outpointed. So no. She lets rip, she storms, she
stalks out—and she makes her point. The managerial mind—
the collective managerial mind—noting this behavior from
various box-office eyries around the world, might condemn it
as childish or prima-donnaish or wearisome or whatever, but
it takes heed, and Callas saves herself the bother of having
to combat a few more awkward or impossible demands in the
future.

As her mother points out, with the hard common
sense that too few people realize goes hand in hand with
Mediterranean emotional volatility, the whole exercise was
undertaken in what the singer regarded as the interests of
her music, and it is salutary to note that in those same interests the true prima donna can exercise the greatest of restraint. Like the time in 1964, when Callas was rehearsing
Tosca and her wig caught fire in the flame of a stage candle-
stick. No histrionics then. No *point* in histrionics then. So she
reacted simply by dabbing at the flames with her hand, while
Tito Gobbi helped her to extinguish them, and she went on
singing, concentrating on the music.

THE QUICK LEFT-HAND BOAST TO THE SOLAR PLEXUS

When used pejoratively against those who imagine that by
assuming the behavior of a certain type of star they will
automatically reproduce the quality (and they, heaven knows,
are legion), or against those in professions where emotions
have logically to be kept under firm control, there is more
justification for the term prima-donnaish. But this is only

true if one is sure that the individual kicking up the fuss is not doing it for some carefully calculated professional end.

Think, for instance, of the contempt and loathing incurred by the young Cassius Clay for just such behavior when he first mouthed his way onto the professional boxing scene with his boasts and his predictions and his doggerel—a contempt and loathing he was deliberately courting in order to get himself the publicity that would attract the potential crowds that would in turn attract the acual promoters. Nowadays, almost everyone interested in the man knows just how calculated those outbursts were, how they had been modeled on the behavior of one Gorgeous George. ("I am the World's Greatest Wrestler. I cannot be defeated. I am the Greatest. I am the King. . . . I cannot be defeated. I am the prettiest. I am the greatest!") Even so, there are still many people who, knowing about that, can't understand why Clay, and later Ali, continued those antics long after that particular objective had been reached and he had earned his title fight: antics repeated on such occasions as weigh-in formalities, or on stepping into the ring, or during the fight itself, or at the end of it, when being interviewed about his next fight. Yet all he is doing at such times is applying, if in a greatly amplified way, one of the oldest tricks in the game—indeed, one of the basic fighting mechanisms of animals as well as humans—the psyching of an opponent. José Torres, who himself had been a comparatively undemonstrative champion, is particularly perceptive on this topic. The fear, he tells us, is nearly always there to begin with, ready to be worked upon by a crafty contestant who can manage to keep his own perfectly natural trepidation in check.

It happened to my last opponent. Minutes before the fight he was substituted for by a friend of mine (who happened to be there wishing me luck . . .).

§ 84 §

The problem had started at the weigh-in ceremony. My rival, after first taking a good look at me, complained of a bad right arm. Then he said it was his left one. The closer I got to him, the more pains and illnesses were uncovered. I knew what was going on. I had often felt the same way when younger, but had had control over my feelings. By fight time my rival had a bad case of diarrhea. I hadn't intended to go that far, but I had literally scared the shit out of him.

Torres doesn't say what his positive contribution to that state of affairs had been on that occasion, but elsewhere he describes in some detail the successful psyching of the very experienced champion Willie Pastrano.

. . . the Garden, after days of negotiation, agreed to play the Puerto Rican National Anthem. My trainer was in front of me and I asked him to move out. I wanted Pastrano to see me singing the anthem with that large Puerto Rican crowd. My throat was tight but after a few bars it loosened up and I hit the notes on pitch and my voice was good. I could feel Pastrano's reaction, "If that mother can sing at a time like this, he's going to be killing me in two minutes."

If such a mild-seeming gentlemanly boxer as Torres could produce such devastation by these tactics, it isn't difficult to realize what havoc a man like Ali can cause. And not only by turning fear into terror. Sometimes the effect aimed at and, in Ali's case, nearly always produced has been to madden the opponent. As Torres suggests, "he made them street fighters again who had to try to 'kill' him by connecting with his seldom-touched face. He must have created an anger which made one feel like breaking his jaw in different places at the same time." As a fellow black, Torres can speak feelingly about this. Pointing out that Ali is never very successful in this approach with white fighters—sometimes not even attempting to use it—he goes on to say:

For Muhammad Ali understands the black man in this country. That's why he psychs them. Ali goes to the root of his people, their culture, their customs, their suffering, their superstitions. It is a profound knowledge of many things that have to do with blacks. Because he understands them and can penetrate their thoughts, they become easier to defeat.

Only occasionally does Ali bungle this aspect of his work, as in his 1971 fight with Frazier. Here his clowning (never very successful in its ability to shake the temperamentally stolid Frazier anyway) took on a somewhat desperate character in the third round, with grins for the crowd, exaggerated shakes of the head, and slaps and an outthrust tongue for his opponent. And not only was it wasted on the champion, but it could also have damaged Ali's chances with the judges. As Torres pointed out: "He is alienating them. Ali is contributing to their natural prejudices. Don't forget, in the Ali-Bonavena fight the money man was Ali. Now he is not the future money man. He's not as far as Madison Square Garden is concerned."

"CRETINS!...SOME OF YOU..."

One principal objective of the calculated outburst or emotional display is to achieve certain ends with others. We have noted it in its raw state, as used by an actual prima donna, and in various aspects when projected by two very clever boxers. It can be effective as a general deterrent (to make people think twice before bugging one with awkward demands); it can be effective as a confidence- or equilibrium-shaking force; and it can even be effective by creating a repulsion that paradoxically attracts the crowds.

Closely linked with the prima donna's general deterrent is the less spectacular version employed by some people—not always in a professional context—with the limited aim of preventing the recurrence, or too frequent recurrence, of a certain kind of annoyance. Even the generally mild-mannered Henry James could resort to this, it seems, when it came to the exasperations and possible dangers of interruption to his writing. Here is a former parlormaid on the subject:

> He was, what shall I say, he was quite all right, but at times —well, when he was on a book, you'd hardly dare to speak to him. He was normally very pleasant, but he got irritable when people worried him and he wanted to write; when you lived in the same house with him you got used to it; his work was the one thing he lived for. Sometimes people called when he was like this, and I didn't dare tell him, and I sent them away. When interrupted during his work he would shout.*

That there was an element of calculation in this seems obvious—not only from the evidence of his social demeanor generally (Henry James? *Shouting?!*)—but also from what one of his secretaries is able to tell us about his reaction when interrupted during dictation on one occasion. There was a knock at the door, a roar from the Master, and in came his manservant with a telegram, trembling with alarm. But when James read it the roar was transformed into a purr: "Lady Maud Warrender asks if I can give her luncheon. She thinks of buying Leasam. What a good thing that would be for Rye! I must see Mrs Paddington [his housekeeper] at once. Miss Weld, will you see to the flowers?"

Like the general deterrent, this type of protective outburst is used as a future time- or trouble-saver. It is used as such by people in all kinds of professions, but particularly

* This and the next anecdote quoted from *Henry James at Home* by H. Montgomery Hyde.

§ 87 §

in those where the work demands high concentration or is conducted under high pressure. It is, in effect, a private localized exercise of the prima donna technique, and unless confined to this area it can cause more trouble than it is worth. I am thinking now of the occasions when it is used in public—where, say, a golfer acquires a reputation for spectacular wrath with gallery fidgeters when he is trying to sink a difficult putt. Well, all right. But he should remember that these people are neither servants nor relatives, and that his behavior can attract exhibitionists and other nuts into deliberately provoking such displays, eventually to his real fury and consequent loss of concentration. And even in private, where regular subordinates are concerned, an individual should learn to temper his outbursts with tact, if the people in question are rather more associates than servants. Barbirolli, for example, was renowned, as many conductors are, for his fulminations at rehearsal. But:

Barbirolli did not insult individual players—he believed that was not the way to get the best of them. His strictures were made to the room in general. "Cretins!" was a favorite word of abuse. But when he had castigated them for their errors and omissions he would add: "Some of you." This became a byword with the Hallé. . . . The Italian in him sometimes made him difficult for English players to work with. Some piece of bad playing would cause him to flare in anger and castigate the recalcitrant section—"playing like *kids*." A second later, when the less volatile English were still simmering with resentment, he would turn on them a smiling face and ask for some exquisite piece of phrasing. . . . While uttering his generalisations his eye would rest on one particular player. "But, Sir, it wasn't me." "What! Did I say it was?" "No, but you *looked* at me." "Well, hell, I've got to look somewhere, haven't I?"*

* From *Barbirolli: Conductor Laureate* by Michael Kennedy.

A MEASURE OF RESTRAINT

We have so far been dealing with the objective aspect of the controlled outburst, which is very important in this context, with a side-glance at the subjective, tension-easing, letting-off-steam aspect, which is really more a sanctioned withdrawal of control, of relatively minor importance. Underlying both, however, is the clamping-down element without which the others would be meaningless—the purely negative ability to restrain one's natural emotional tendencies, especially at times of crisis. In professions where the crises tend to be long-drawn-out, or where minor crises tend to come in series of the one-damn-thing-after-another variety, this negative ability is of supreme importance: the element that makes for fruitful intelligent persistence that is always so much more effective than mere blind stubbornness, useful though the latter may be.

Brunel offered a splendid example of this when confronted with what seemed to be an insurmountable problem: that of getting his ship the *Great Britain* afloat after it had run aground on the Irish coast on sand that concealed rocks. Inundated with problems arising from some of his other enterprises, he was able to spare the time for only a brief inspection, during which he noted the ineffectuality of the salvage attempts. This produced one of his rare outbursts of anger, but one that did much to galvanize into activity the people on the spot. Here is how it was expressed in a letter to the captain of the ship, which Brunel declared to be in perfect shape:

. . . except that at one part the bottom is much bruised and knocked in holes in several places. . . . There is some slight damage to [the stern], not otherwise important than as pointing out the necessity for some precautions if she is to be saved. I say "if", for really when I saw a vessel still in perfect condition left to the tender mercies of an awfully exposed shore for weeks, while a parcel of quacks are amusing you with schemes for getting her off, she in the meantime being left to go to pieces, I could hardly help feeling as if her own parents and guardians meant her to die there. . . .

He then went on to the practicalities, advising protective measures until the following spring, when the weather would be more favorable for salvage operations. These measures consisted in the stacking of large bundles of twigs and small branches, lashed together with iron rods and weighted with iron and sandbags, under the stern of the vessel and halfway up her length on the ocean side: "just like a huge poultice." With Brunel not there to supervise the operation, however, it did not go at all well. The seas persistently washed away the foundations of the "poultice" and Captain Claxton, after persevering for some time, wrote a despairing account to Brunel. Now the captain was a determined, experienced man himself—a good regular pro in fact. But Brunel was a super-pro, and his reply shows the distinction with great clarity:

You have failed, I think, in sinking and keeping down the fagots from that which causes nine-tenths of all failures in this world, from not doing quite enough. . . . I would only impress upon you one principle of action which I have always found very successful, which is to stick obstinately to one plan (until I believe it wrong), and to devote all my scheming to that one plan and, on the same principle, to stick to one method and push that to the utmost limits before I allow myself to wander into others; in fact, to use a simile, to stick to the one point of attack, however defended, and if the force first brought up is not sufficient, to bring ten times as much; but never to try back upon another in the hope of finding it easier. So with the fagots—if a six-bundle fagot won't reach out of the water, try a twenty-bundle one; if hundredweights won't keep it down, try tons.

And it worked.

§ 90 §

This was of course more than obstinacy. This was persistence arising out of the control of despair—and a despair not only of the possibility of overcoming the mighty natural forces he was up against, but also of the possibility of conquering the powerful human difficulties involved, of overriding the effects of other people's succumbing to the first kind of despair. This victory is all the more laudable in that Brunel was not by nature a stoical man, but vivacious, sensitive, volatile—typically Gallic, one might have said, remembering the French father. Yet to succeed in his profession the control had to be acquired; and his ambition and pride and faith in himself combined to ensure that it was. Self-faith: it might almost be treated as a separate ingredient of superprofessionalism, something much more fundamental than self-confidence, which has to be acquired along with emotional control, and sometimes simulated. A comment of Brunel's biographer, L. T. C. Rolt, serves to underline the point: "This unshakable faith in himself, though he sometimes suspected it to be the sin of pride, schooled him during this time of adversity [in the early days of his career] to hide his feelings behind a bold front of self-confidence and enthusiasm which impressed everyone he met and which, aside from his remarkable abilities, contributed more than anything else to his ultimate success."

This business of dissembling—the outward, the *export* aspect of the control of one's emotions—is of great importance to professionals of all kinds. Machiavelli rated it a high place in the essential armory of princes, pouring scorn on Appius for his neglect of the art, pointing out that the tyrant did not do at all well

in suddenly changing his character from that of friend of the plebs to that of an open enemy, from being humane to being arrogant, from being easy going to being difficult; and in doing this so quickly that no one had any excuse for failing to recognize the crookedness of his mind. For he who has at one time seemed to be good, and proposes for his own purposes to become bad, should make the change by appropriate stages, so adapting his conduct to circumstances that, before the change in character has robbed you of your old supporters, it may have brought you so many new ones that your power will not be lessened.

Conversely, Machiavelli was able to praise Junius Brutus for the control he was able to apply to his playing the fool, not only as a purely defensive means of preserving his estates, but also "in order to escape observation and that he might get a better opportunity of downing the kings and liberating his country . . ." Restraint, indeed, is one of the paramount virtues in the Machiavellian universe, even though in passing he could grant a place to strong emotional involvement where the common troops were concerned (always more reliable than mercenaries—"for they have no cause to stand firm when attacked, apart from the small pay which you give them"). Here he is on the subject of the valuable restraining influence of restraint itself:

. . . nothing is more suitable to restrain an excited crowd than respect for some man of gravity and standing who in person confronts them. Hence not without reason does Virgil say:

> If then some grave and pious man appear
> They hush their noise and lend a listening ear.

This being so, a person who has command of an army or who finds himself in a city where a tumult has arisen should present himself before those involved with as much grace and dignity as he can muster. . . .

A course of action too frequently avoided in the tumultuous cities of the modern world, one feels, apart from places like

New York, where, if not with complete dignity then certainly with a telling sort of grace, Mayor Lindsay employed it to good effect in recent years.

But this is only the tactical aspect. Machiavelli—and here he sheds his cloak of cynicism and makes a positive affirmation—could not set too high a value on the control that manifests itself in equanimity: equanimity in victory as well as in defeat, in good times and in bad.

Among the other splendid things which our historian makes Camillus say and do in order to show how an outstanding man should behave he puts into Camillus' mouth these words: "The dictatorship did not elate me, nor did exile depress me." One sees here how great men remain the same whatever befalls. If fortune changes, sometimes raising them, sometimes casting them down, they do not change, but remain ever resolute, so resolute in mind and in conduct throughout life that it is easy for anyone to see that fortune holds no sway over them. Not so do weak men behave; for by good fortune they are buoyed up and intoxicated, and ascribe such success as they meet with, to a virtue they never possessed, so that they become insupportable and odious to all who have anything to do with them. This then brings about a sudden change in their lot, the prospect of which causes them to go to the other extreme and to become base and abject. Hence it comes about that rulers so built prefer to run away rather than to defend themselves in adversity, just as do men who find themselves defenseless because they have misused the good fortune they had.

Emotional restraint, of course, is the only answer to the sort of calculated-insult campaign discussed earlier in relation to championship fighting. (And while on the subject so soon after Machiavelli's noble pronouncement, let us be careful not to mistake mere cockiness or dissembled bravado for the unthinking intoxication in victory that he talks about. Ali, for all his braggadocio, just has to be one of the most equanimous of superprofessionals for his talents to have survived the enormous distractions involved in the stripping of his title, the withholding of his license, and the threat—drawn out over several years—of a long term of imprisonment.) But while it is one thing to restrain one's anger at some blatantly obvious tactical attempt to provoke it—an attempt rarely sustained for more than the few weeks before a contest—it is something else again to keep one's temper when an onslaught of insults or petty frustrations is kept up for months or even years at a time. Such massive attacks, wave after wave of them, had to be endured by Florence Nightingale, and it is well worth examining in detail this aspect of her Crimean experiences.

THE LADY WITH THE CLAMP

On her arrival at Scutari with her first party of nurses, Miss Nightingale had been ignored by the doctors there. The British Ambassador to Turkey, Lord Stratford, was favorably disposed to the project but too lazy and too indifferent to the plight of the soldiers even to visit the hospitals, let alone help sort out the difficulties the party found itself in. But, with the administrative tactical shrewdness already mentioned, Florence Nightingale bided her time. Determined not to press the matter into open conflict, she opted for waiting until the doctors should become so overwhelmed with work as to ask for her nurses' assistance. This period lasted for weeks, with the women's duties being confined to preparing bandages and bed linen, and to cooking special diets (to be supplied only on the express requisition of the medical staff). Not until winter set in and the stream of casualties became a flood did the doctors relent, as Miss Nightingale had hoped. Then she and her nurses were able to justify their presence and establish their position—but gradually, cautiously, never doing anything without the medical staff's approval, a position that brought Miss Nightingale into conflict from time to time with various warmhearted but ingenuous nurses and helpers. And gradually too she began to acquire allies even among the doctors.

Then came the first major setback. With little warning and contrary to her earlier instructions, a party of forty more nurses was sent out, headed by her friend Mary Stanley. Not only did this cause a terrible quartering crisis (there had hardly been room for the original party), but since this new move had been made without the medical staff's approval either, the whole delicate diplomatic balance that had been so patiently achieved was put into jeopardy. Miss Nightingale was furious. She fired off a searing letter to her friend Sydney Herbert, the man responsible—a letter that in its fury fully justified the epithet "unbridled" and showed how great her control was when it really counted. To make matters worse, there was the fact that the new party contained a strong Roman Catholic element, thus upsetting another painfully achieved balance at a time when sectarian rivalries were so bitter as to override completely the basic humanitarian considerations. Moreover, the fifteen Irish nuns in the new detachment felt themselves to be under the command only of their Superior, Mother Bridgeman, who in turn acknowledged the authority only of her Bishop—a truly Lowell-Cabot-God situation in a context where it could do real damage, with many lives at stake.

The quartering problem imposed itself immediately. There was simply nowhere to put the new party. Furthermore, the money it had set out with had been squandered during the journey, and Miss Nightingale had to lend them £390 out of her own pocket for their immediate necessities.

To Mary Stanley herself she made no secret of her wrath.
And yet, as her biographer, Cecil Woodham-Smith, points
out:

. . . harassed and distracted as she was, when her first anger was
over she saw that it would be disastrous to send the party back.
Racial and religious issues were involved, and Lord Napier had
gone so far as to say that in his opinion there would be almost
a rebellion in Ireland if the Irish nuns under Mother Bridgeman
were sent home. A scandal would do the cause she had at heart
irreparable harm. She must swallow her grievance.

So she suggested a compromise, sending home some of the
sectarian nurses from the first party, replacing them with the
Irish nuns, and promising to try to place some of the others
in the new convalescence hospitals due to be opened shortly.
    Surviving the public sectarian storm that this still pro-
voked wasn't easy, and although it eventually blew itself out
and the position was made less difficult by the Medical Officer's being persuaded to accept an enlarged nursing staff,
Mother Bridgeman continued to make trouble and Mary
Stanley continued to make life exasperating with her combined ineffectuality and her socialite-level friendship with
the ambassador's wife. Even when Miss Stanley and the Irish
nuns contrived to get themselves a hospital of their own,
away from Scutari, their conduct was such that it damaged
the image of nursing and the respect for it that Florence
Nightingale had been trying so hard to establish, and . . . so
on. One damned, one double-damned thing after another—
with more and more casualties pouring in, and Miss Nightingale venting her anger privately but keeping it tightly
under control when dealing with those chiefly responsible,
the authorities, and working, working, working until she

made herself ill and had to keep her reactions to *that* under control, too.

But there was more. With the winter over, the ensuing lull in the casualty rate brought no relief to her exasperations and frustrations, for then the departmental jealousies and suspicions were revived. Worse, the sadistic and professionally substandard Dr. John Hall, Chief of the Crimea Medical Staff, was able to turn his baleful attentions to the hospitals at base. One of his first moves was to appoint an acknowledged, a publicly reprimanded, incompetent to the post of Senior Medical Officer at the main Barracks Hospital—a puppet through whom he could begin to snipe at Miss Nightingale with all the considerable flair for behind-the-scenes intrigue he could command. Still she kept control of her feelings, so successfully as to survive the first onslaught and get the Barracks Hospital into a sufficiently satisfactory state for her to move on to the General Hospital at Balaclava, from which she'd had some disturbing news about the nurses' professional conduct. But this move only gave Hall his chance to undermine her authority even further, and she went with what amounted to his encouragement to the staff there to snub her, even to treat her with open hostility.

The result? Still the control. She set about putting right some of the most obvious deficiencies. Then she collapsed and fell seriously ill. The British commander, Lord Raglan, visited her sickbed, expressing deep concern, and this looked like being of immense value to her in her battle with Hall. But then, very soon after the visit, Lord Raglan died, to be succeeded by a far less sympathetic general. Things came to such a pitch that at the end of the year, when no official statement came to establish her authority:

. . . Dr. Hall gave out that she was an adventuress and to be treated as such. Minor officials treated her with vulgar impertinence. The Purveyor refused to honour her drafts. When she went to the General Hospital, she was kept waiting.

"But she would not be provoked," states her biographer, Woodham-Smith, and that is the theme that runs throughout this episode of her life, with the matter of her authority not being cleared up positively and conclusively until well into the following year. "They are killing me!" she told her "Aunt" Mai, who came to stay with her. "The victory is lost already." Her visitor was appalled at the state of her health and living conditions. She wrote: "Food, rest, temperature never interfere with her doing her work. You would be surprised at the temperature in which she lives . . . she who suffers so much from cold. . . . She has attained a most wonderful calm. No irritation of temper, no hurry or confusion of manner ever appears for a moment."

In short it was an application of that modern precept—well-known in the Ali/Torres world and other sections far removed from nursing: "Don't get mad, get even." Florence Nightingale surely demonstrated the policy more vividly, and in greater depth, and over longer periods, than anyone else on record.

Yet as I have hinted in an earlier chapter, there was possibly a deeper force at work here—something indifferent to effectiveness—a force to which those phrases, those *cris de coeur,* "They are killing me!" and "The victory is lost already," seem to offer clues. At face value those are the words of someone who has been beaten, who is genuinely at the point of surrender. But Miss Nightingale's behavior, her persistence—her intelligent, patient, facts-weighing, points-watching persistence—belied such "convictions" even as she uttered them. So that in the last analysis we are forced to ask ourselves if there might not have been in Florence Nightingale's personality a strong vein of masochism.

§ 98 §

OF PRICKS AND KICKS

Masochism—harnessed and applied, whether fully consciously or not—seems to be part of the equipment of many super-professionals. We have noted it in the openly gloating terms with which Kepler described his almost Sisyphean labors. There is something about the rhapsodic element in the notes Henry James made at the time of the theatre debacle that points in the same direction. And among other examples already quoted in this study, one notes a certain eagerness in Stanislavski to describe and dwell upon his early short-comings that is in excess of their purely illustrative and cautionary value.

We shall be dealing at length later with the subject of attention to detail, and particularly the aspect of taking pains —of painstaking thoroughness and the "infinite capacity for taking pains" that some people think is the only prescription for excellence—but in the present context it is worth noting that the very phrase, "the taking of pains," could be regarded as synonymous with "masochism." Was there perhaps some such link between Ernest Hemingway's tendency to revel in his wounds and his habit of massively cutting and altering his copy well into the proof stages? (This could of course have included an element of sadism as far as his publishers were concerned, as they tried to cope with this expensive habit.) Do many writers not make rather too much of a display of their willingness to chop and change and sweat blood this way? And then there is the question of sensitivity to criticism: not only Hemingway's, which was pathological and notorious, but also that of many other great writers. Leonard Woolf used to complain, with the logic and something of the bewilderment of the well-balanced man that he was, of the contrast between his wife's fleeting pleasure in good reviews of her books and the lasting pain she allowed even the most trivial of the bad ones to inflict upon her. But the significant thing is that such reviews never cause victims of Virginia Woolf's or Hemingway's kind to falter much, let alone give in altogether, as they did the British novelist mentioned earlier, who took them so much to heart as to despair of ever reaching the new generation. And however much the masochistically inclined may howl with rage or weep with fury at these scratches, they continue to ask for more (unlike some of the more healthily minded of the hurt ones, who don't give in either, but who take care after a while never to read their notices, or have them presorted and read only the good ones)—to hire themselves out for more, to use Hemingway's phrase—as if stimulated by the smarting of their own salt tears on encountering the lacerations.

Not all superpros have this tendency, of course; maybe not even a majority. It is not absolutely essential. But if one has it and can control it, it can make life easier. In the opinion of some it is even worth simulating, or acquiring through the habit of simulation. "You don't know misfortune!" said Eleanora Duse, criticizing an actor during rehearsal. "If you don't you must find it. Tell yourself that you are unfortunate and you will see how your acting improves. I do it well because I carry bitterness within me."

In some fields an element of masochism is obviously more useful than in others—in boxing, for instance, where, apart from the necessity to sweat and agonize over the perfection of one's skills and to undergo privations in training, there is the obligation to absorb a more than customary amount of actual physical pain. Certainly there is nothing of the masochist in Ali, say, with his passionate (and wholly natural) concern for avoiding disfiguring punishment, but one feels he is very much a rarity in this respect. Yet for those who do have the tendency *and can control it* (those who can't soon end up as punching bags), it must be an invaluable asset when facing clever and tough opponents. For one thing, it can help a man to overcome frustration. Torres seems to have summed it up when he says: "The only real alternative to continued frustration is guts, heart, balls—'cojones'— which means, 'I'm not going to quit. I won't make it easy for him.' The will to win begins to disappear; the balls to stay on your feet remains"—but I think we may now add to that that a touch of masochism can help too. And for another thing it can help with the psyching where the psyching counts double—in the ring—by *inducing* frustration in an opponent. Torres again:

If you hit a man with your best shot, and he doesn't flinch, the thing to do is to keep hitting him until he falls. You have to keep doing it until the last second of the last round. Even if he still is not flinching, you might still have won the fight. But usually, when a man is hitting another man hard and continuously and the other man simply smiles and keeps coming at him, the man throwing the punches suffers. He can get discouraged, his will easily can leave him.

Machismo—pride, ego—can be of great service to the smiler here, surely. But let us not forget the potency of machismo's near-anagram, which can put a devastating conviction into that smile—and not only as it is applied to boxing but to all other professions. Indeed, one might summarize this topic and introduce the next by saying that so much frustration, so much exasperation, so much essential opposition, so many blowpipe darts and so many blowfly droppings come the superpro's way that he'd better get to welcome them, if only wryly, if only as signs that he's still alive and to be reckoned with. "Knocks" Persons, the engaging Harlem racketeer of Ernest Tidyman's *Shaft* novels, clearly had this in mind when paying a visit to a rival outside his own territory.

6

Coming Back— and Going Beyond

You are a professional golfer. You are driving your car along a highway at night and collide with a bus. You are badly hurt but it is an hour and a half before an ambulance arrives, and then there is a journey of 150 miles to be made before you get into a hospital. There the doctors find that you have fractured a shoulder, your pelvis, and an ankle. (And you are a professional golfer.) The bones are set. You wait. You hope. Then a blood clot develops. There is a danger that it may reach the heart. The doctors decided to operate on one of the major veins.

Days and nights of delirium follow, but you survive. A month after the operation you are discharged from hospital. You weigh just under a hundred pounds. Your muscles are so weak that you have to regain your ability to walk a literal few steps at a time. And since you are(?)/were(?) a professional golfer, you go around to the local club after a month or so, and do some of your walking there, with friends, a few holes at a time. And you start to exercise your arm muscles with a few swings at a time. Not until nine or ten months after your accident are you fit enough to *play* a few holes. But you *are* a professional golfer, no doubt about it, and in the next few weeks you keep on practicing, and you feel you're doing so well that you decide to try yourself out by entering for the Los Angeles Open. Everybody is surprised that you're even trying at this level so soon, but their surprise turns to amazement when you go on to score 73–69–69–69 and so tie with one of the great champions of all time: Sam Snead.

But then that is what the subject was himself: Ben Hogan, superprofessional, the man who went on to win the U.S. Open twice in the next five years. And what he was displaying was one of the superpro's most important single qualities —the one they really must possess—the ability to survive disappointment and defeat that is so powerful as to translate itself, if necessary, into the ability to overcome disease and disaster.

The ability to survive disappointment and defeat, though less dramatic, is the aspect that chiefly concerns us here, for while a superprofessional may or may not become involved in an accident, and may or may not be afflicted with a crippling illness, he will certainly encounter setbacks in his career, sometimes singly, sometimes in clusters. Indeed, the chances are that a single disappointment will, if severe enough, trigger off a cluster, because of its tendency to create anxiety or frustration, which can then result in loss of concentration or rhythm, which in turn leads to loss of confidence and general form, and more disappointments. Naturally, such a progression, or regression, is more likely to happen in the case of a young professional, before he has learned how to handle the situation sufficiently well to check its cumulative effect at an early stage; but sometimes, due to a run of bad circumstances out of his control, a superpro at the very peak of his powers will be similarly afflicted.

How then *is* the situation handled? How does the super-pro set about restoring the self-confidence, rhythms, concentration, and so on? There are in fact several ways, depending on such factors as the type of profession, the nature of the damage, and, above all, the personality and age of the subject. But there seems to be one principle that is basic to them all: that while stars may lose self-confidence, they must never lose faith in their powers and abilities. As Fritz Kreisler put it, when giving encouragement to Barbirolli during the latter's trying early years with the New York Philharmonic: "An artist must believe in himself and mustn't be easily swayed. A public man must take whatever comes to him." To lose that self-belief or self-faith is to lose hope—and that means an early retirement, or a permanent switch to another profession, or suicide, or some other form of capitulation. That is what distinguishes self-faith from self-confidence. For while you can't have self-confidence without faith in yourself, you can still retain faith in yourself when going through a period of loss of confidence. Or, to put it another way: a man with self-faith can go through a bad patch, admitting he is off form, and still say: "But I know I am good, that this *is* only a bad patch, and that even though my self-confidence has been weakened it will certainly return to full vigor." A man who can say that has already taken one step on the way back. It means he will not be readily trapped into courting more disappointments by trying too hard too soon to redress the balance. It means that even if his personality is the sort to express itself in bombast or bitterness, in threats to hang up his boots or burn his canvases, in declarations of intent to enter a monastery or emigrate to Australia or become a publisher (a favorite with disgruntled authors), the damage is not permanent, the healing work is in progress.

But how is this faith preserved—particularly in periods when everything seems to conspire to shake it, to sow the suspicion that maybe, after all, one has been suffering from delusions about the nature of one's abilities? A touch of megalomania helps, of course. If you are a lunatic, and you believe you're the greatest painter ever, and you do happen to have great talent, you're untouchable. And, as we have seen, a streak of masochism can do much to make the stings and cuts endurable. (Or even enjoyable—as Sir Richard Burton had to confess when writing about the return from one of his successful expeditions: "I had time, on the top of my mule for musing upon how melancholy a thing is success. Whilst failure inspirits a man, attainment reads the sad prosy lesson that all our glories 'Are shadows not substantial things.' Truly said the sayer, 'disappointment is the salt of life'—a salutary bitter which strengthens the mind for fresh exertion, and gives a double value to the prize.") Or, going to the other extreme, the coldly sane mind, trained in the Machiavellian virtue of equanimity in success as well as failure, will have less difficulty than most in preserving self-faith during bad patches.

But for the superpro with less extreme emotional tendencies, the steps to be taken to ensure his bending rather than breaking have to be more positive and deliberate. And one of the most obvious directions he might take is along the line of research—which brings us back in the company of the Westminster gardener, whose erudition, one may be sure, often stood him in good stead when confronted with the blackfly and the rust, the mildew and the canker, and other setbacks. For the value of such researches lies not only in suggesting remedies for faults that have been found in one's own performance, or for the ills that have afflicted it through no fault of one's own, but also—and this is even more important—in pointing out that great predecessors have suffered in similar ways and survived.

Another way of dealing with the setback situation is to rely on the cushioning effect of sympathy emanating from those around one. This could come from the sort of comradely group we find cropping up in the lives of painters—particularly in Europe: the companions-in-arms-and-in-distress kind of circle, usually of a revolutionary nature, within which defeat and disappointment at the hands of the outside world can be alchemized into honorable victory. Such a cushioning works well so long as the profession involved lends itself to this kind of semimilitant grouping and so long as the individual remains at one with its spirit and aims. But sooner or later this is likely to fail him, whereupon he may find himself relying in times of distress on the more general cushioning supplied by coaches, managers, or agents on the strictly professional level, by the retinue of hangers-on on the subprofessional level, or by the close relatives and old friends on the purely personal plane. Any or all of these will be performing a vital service if they can convince the slapped-down superpro that he still has talent. Not necessarily, be it noted, their love or admiration. The "there's-one-little-lad-who-calls-me-dad-shake-hands-with-a-millionaire" kind of consolation doesn't work at this level. The best of such morale-boosting agents know by instinct or by observation and deduction and experience where the root of the matter lies, and they will go to work accordingly. They will know the right precedents to quote; they will know when and when not to hark back to the wounded one's past successes; they will know the value of reminding him of past defeats and the ways he triumphed over them eventually. But how they perform this vital function—how they help to convince him that he has *not* lost his talent—and whether they do it for love or money, hardly matters so long as they succeed. And those who are able to succeed, if necessary time and time again, surely qualify for the accolade of superprofessionals themselves, as I have suggested earlier, for it is in itself an art commensurate with that of the psychiatrist, and a job that involves great skill, tact, finesse, and persistence.

The danger of this remedy lies in its possible breakdown, which can bring on the final catastrophe. It was a situation beloved by the old Hollywood, particularly in its show-biz screen biographies, though nonetheless true for all that. I am thinking of those scenes wherein the Great One's despair and the tantrums reflecting it finally wear down the patience of wife or lover and professional aide alike. "I can't stand this any longer!" blurts the one, walking out of his life and so adding to his troubles, either directly or through remorse. "You're all washed up, buddy!" snarls the other, nursing the place where the star has slugged him in a fit of pique, and at the same time touching with less tenderness but great professional accuracy the core of the other's deepest wound.

Naturally a big enough and sufficiently assorted retinue can help toward averting such a catastrophe, but there are safer if perhaps slower methods of ensuring the preservation of faith in oneself. Retreat is one of them. Here the victim hastens to cut himself off from the noises and reverberations, the fallout and the debris of his downfall, including the shallow commiserations which can be just as destructive as the jeers. Usually it is a retreat in the physical sense—a getting-the-hell-out-of-it to a place where the subject has a chance to think through the circumstances without distraction and to plan his recovery accordingly. Without primary *associated* distraction, that is, for the secondary distractions of background detail—the change of scenery and life-style with all the minor readjustments and decisions involved—can help to soothe the subject in the early days, before he is out of shock. One thinks in this connection of Henry James leaving London and the scene of his theatrical humiliation and fussing over the details of his new home in Rye, details concerning furniture, servants, garden shrubs, and neighbors.

Sometimes, however, the chosen retreat will be nongeographical. The subject will simply shrug off the recent defeat, no matter how numbed by it he may be still, and plunge straightaway along some other different line of action, equally or almost equally dear to his heart. This policy of diversification is of course likely to be successful only with those lucky enough to be genuinely multitalented, or those whose single profession embraces many widely divergent branches—for example, writing, which can be applied to several different media. Thus a Cocteau can switch from making films to writing poetry, or from painting murals to devising a new ballet. Or a Hemingway may turn from writing novels to concocting a magazine story, or from that to reporting a bullfight or a battle. It is not necessary that such people be equally good at the alternatives open to them— just good enough to make their participation felt, to have a hope of achieving critical acclaim or gaining high financial reward, and, above all, to involve them in concentrated effort. Thus will deep wounds have a chance to heal naturally, when fingers that might be overinclined to probe nervously or morbidly, or to pull aside the dressing or pick at the scab too soon, are otherwise engaged. Among the many who have used this method successfully, if in different ways and with different intensities, one might quote Sarah Bernhardt and her sculpturing, Frank Sinatra and his acting, and our old cool calculating friend, Isambard Kingdom Brunel.

THREE DIVERSIFIERS

With Bernhardt, her sculpturing was much more than a hobby to which she could turn for mild solace in times of trouble, yet rather less than a second vocation. She was sufficiently involved to devote long periods of time to it, but only when things became too hot for her to continue in her frequently stormy acting career. And while she was talented enough to win honorable mentions for her sculpture and make a substantial income from the sales, it never reached the heights of acclaim that her acting did. Yet instinctively she realized the pursuit's value as a refuge, and used it as such, so that while there may have been some truth in her detractors' claim that she was using her sculpturing for its publicity value rather than as a source of artistic satisfaction, there was always this other dimension. Moreover, as an actress of the very highest caliber, she was able to bring to her endeavors in this field a conviction and intensity that would have been impossible, say, for a lesser actress or a writer or a businesswoman. As Henry Knepler has pointed out:

Her studio was scenery, a dramatic setting for the sculptress, rather than a useful workroom. It had its bohemian aspects, but mainly it strove to be the perfect studio, the perfect setting for the artist. In it Sarah wore the perfect clothes, which may have been less perfect to work in—a white blouse or vest, and white trousers, all made of silk, adorned with a large lace collar and cuffs, and rounded out with a white tulle cravat.*

Bernhardt's retreats into the studio were largely retreats from temporary difficulties rather than major crises involving her faith in herself as an actress, although one feels that they

* From *The Gilded Stage.*

would have served their purpose well even in such direr circumstances.

Where Sinatra was concerned, the situation precipitating the switch could hardly have been bleaker. Although he was still an excellent singer of his kind of songs, the vogue for them had temporarily passed, and that recession, plus some bad publicity, seemed to mark the end of his career. What happened to lift him out of those doldrums was the chance to use his acting talent (already exercised in movies that had featured him primarily for his singing) in a straight dramatic role. The result, in *From Here to Eternity,* proved to be so successful as quite to restore his confidence as a singer, as he made supremely evident in so many of his post-*Eternity* albums. The irony of it seems to be that, although going on to consider his acting and moviemaking talents as great as his singing talent, he has frequently failed to do them equal justice. Sheilah Graham has said: "With his craggy, nicked, worked-over face, he could have been another Bogart on the screen . . . if he had given as much attention and concentration to the longer job of making a film as he does to making a record or a television show."* Well, maybe. Or maybe the plain truth is that these secondary talents are just that, secondary to the singing, tremendously valuable props and nothing more.

Brunel's case is different again: that of diversification within a single profession. As we have already noted, he had always been eager as a young man to investigate all aspects of engineering whenever the opportunities presented themselves. Originally, no doubt, this was largely the result of his passionate interest in the work in general, which set up a momentum that almost automatically propelled his attention into so many corners. But soon he began to realize its tactical

* From *Scratch an Actor.*

value, and whereas a more cautious and a less intuitively far-seeing man might have decided to narrow the range of his interests and so conserve his energies, Brunel could appreciate that there was greater safety ultimately in pursuing the same seemingly profligate course. It has been said, as an illustration of his "unshakable faith in himself" that "once one project on which he had pinned his hopes had failed he would rapidly recover from the blow, dismiss it from his mind and concentrate on the next with undiminished energy." Rather, to my mind, is this a *recipe* for the unshakability of that faith, with the recovery from the blow and its dismissal from his mind coming *after* his moving on to the next project. And when it came to one of his really great trials—during the railway recession that followed the downfall of George Hudson, when Brunel was so dispirited as to contemplate withdrawal even to the point of designing his own retirement house—that recipe came to his rescue again. Here, through the medium of his sketchbooks, is how his biographer, L. T. C. Rolt, saw it taking effect:

They show that the same disillusionment with railways which led the private man to contemplate retirement drove the engineer to dwell more and more upon problems of marine engineering. What could be more natural? With England a tom-tiddler's ground of rival railway speculators, the oceans of the world offered far freer scope for a man of his restless temperament. The sketch books faithfully reflect this change of emphasis. Amidst drawings for the new Paddington and station layouts for the broad-gauge route into Birmingham, the eye is suddenly arrested by a sketch of an extraordinary steamship as long as the page is wide and bristling with funnels and masts. It is dated 25 March 1852. The drawing is headed "East India Steamship" and beneath it is scribbled casually the note: "Say 600ft x 65ft x 30ft," dimensions which any contemporary shipwright would have regarded with absolute incredulity. Thereafter the pages of the sketch books are haunted by apparitions of gigantic ships. They appear with different masts and rigs; sometimes with both screws and paddles; sometimes with two sets of paddles.

Brunel, one need hardly add, never completed his plans for the retirement house. He did go on to build such a ship.

FITZGERALD PLAYS THE FIELD

But the diversification method doesn't always work, even when applied within the framework of the one profession. When it fails, the results can be terrible, as in the case of Scott Fitzgerald. In fact, since this writer tried nearly all the methods of preservation of self-faith discussed here, it will be worth looking at his increasingly disaster-ridden career in some detail—beginning, ironically enough, with a course that was extremely successful. It might be described as the Quick Strike-Back, and in Fitzgerald's case and the words of his biographer Andrew Turnbull, operated like this:

His job [his first, as a copywriter] bored him, and he couldn't sell the plays, stories, poems, sketches, lyrics, jokes which he composed in his off hours. Each evening he hurried back to his room to find a rejected manuscript which he immediately mailed to another magazine. Then he wrote something new and sent that off, and concluded his day by getting more or less drunk.

This is essentially a method for the Young Unknown. It has the paramount virtue of keeping alive and increasing his chances of recognition, while at the same time sharpening his skills by persistent regular practice. Loss of faith is still the danger, certainly, but to nothing like the extent that it would be in the case of an older man with an established talent, for at this early stage the subject can console himself with the thought that great talent usually *does* take a while to attract attention, so what the hell? What is more, the danger of loss of faith isn't coupled with an actual loss of face. No rivals or enemies need get to know about these turndowns. There is no publicity attached. So again, what the hell?

And so—because Fitzgerald was at the outset of his career, and his profession was one in which there is always a time lag between performance and result, a time lag during which luck or the successful result of an earlier performance has a chance to manifest itself—the method worked. But later, as he was nearing the dangerous age of forty, when his health was undermined by drink, by the long-drawn-out mental sickness of his wife, and by the falloff in his once tremendous popularity, it was with quite different results that he tried that method again. This time, Turnbull has to describe it thus: ". . . Fitzgerald had been playing roulette with his talent, spinning it recklessly in the hope that something would score, and as his stories became more slapdash, Ober [his agent] was obliged to hold them up for revision."

But this was only one of several methods Fitzgerald tried in his desperation. He sought refuge, and hope, and reassurance, in giving encouragement to protégés: young men who might repay his generous but not altogether unselfish interest by acting as collaborators in writing plays, or as advance salesmen in Hollywood. It came to nothing. Veering back to his basic medium, he aimed at internal diversification in a project for an historical novel—a melodrama set in the ninth century and built around some short stories he'd written for a magazine. Again, nothing. He then dreamed up a plan for giving a series of lectures at Princeton on the art of creating fiction, and even offered to give his services for nothing, so hopeful was he—and probably justifiably so—of its therapeutic and reputation-reviving potential. But the authorities gave him a cool response—no doubt influenced in this by his other, still all-too-thriving reputation as an alcoholic—and again nothing came of it. And so he went careening on, into the "roulette" period already mentioned, and beyond, into a state of near-breakdown.

Fitzgerald's secretary that summer of 1936 remembered his frenzied efforts to write amid fears his talent had deserted him. She remembered the trouble the nurse had getting him to eat, and she remembered coming into his darkened room when he was lying on the bed and saying, "Scott, what is going to become of you?" Staring at the ceiling, he answered quietly, "God knows." He wasn't devoid of self-pity, yet he viewed his life with detachment and blamed himself for his plight.

So detached was he, still so professional as to be able to recognize the cause of the trouble, or at least its deadliest aspect, that he continued to struggle, as predicted by a fellow author who visited him around this time and reported back to his anxious editor: "I do not think you need to worry about him, physically or psychologically. He has thrown himself on the floor and shrieked himself black in the face and pounded his heels—as lots of us do in one way or another—but when it's over he'll go back to his building blocks again." And so he did, managing to get himself dried out and fit enough to undertake yet another, this time more sustained, exercise in diversification: a general scriptwriting contract with MGM.

Fitzgerald approached this with a certain tough humility—and high hopes. He aimed at mastering the job from the ground up, having persuaded himself that the movies had superseded the novel as "the strongest and supplest medium for conveying thought and emotion from one human being to another." There was a certain very sensible prophylactic element in this attitude in that it enabled him to dismiss his unpleasant memories of previous scriptwriting experiences as of little account, for then he had been a successful novelist working on the adaptation of his own books, a creature quite different from a potential great screenplay writer in his own right. Unfortunately, however, he was still in reality too much of a novelist—indeed, too great a novelist, artistically too splendid an isolationist—to operate efficiently in such an essentially collaborative field as moviemaking. Inside two years, drinking heavily, he was back in hospital, spinning his short-story roulette again, but still with a stubborn finger on the trouble spot.

I have been paying the grocer with short pieces for Esquire, meanwhile trying to get the detachment from physical and mental worries which is necessary for a good short story. . . . I have many times wished that my work was of a mechanical sort that could be done or delegated irrespective of morale, for I don't want or expect happiness for myself—only enough peace to keep us all going.

And, not long after, he could write:

I am not a great man, but sometimes I think the impersonal and objective quality of my talent and the sacrifices of it, in pieces, to preserve its essential value has some sort of epic grandeur.

His talent and its preservation: no wonder there were tears in his eyes sometimes when he spoke of it. For, as Andrew Turnbull says, "His talent was his lifeline." And in the end he triumphed, in that it was his heart that gave out, not his faith. Indeed, in one sense it may be said that his diversification efforts succeeded after all, for with the collapse of his scriptwriting ambitions he turned back with all the greater face-saving, nose-thumbing determination to straight novel-writing (always his true fictional métier, incidentally, rather than the short story) and it was while he was at work on *The Last Tycoon*—happily, busily, soberly, carefully, and, above all, confidently—that he died.

WORKING IT OUT

Which brings us to what is probably the strongest and most reliable faith-preserver of all: work—work that is within one's special province rather than at its periphery or beyond. Fitzgerald realized this at last, writing to his daughter that he wished he'd never relaxed or looked back after *The Great Gatsby* but had said: "I've found my line—from now on this comes first. This is my immediate duty—without this I am nothing." He would still have gone through painful and distressing times, no doubt. Nothing he wrote could have saved his wife's sanity or averted the circumstances that contributed to the temporary revolution in the taste of the general novel reader. But he would have found earlier, along with his "line," that continued work in the field could bring its own form of backhanded consolation. As Bertrand Russell has said:

> The power to produce great art is often, though by no means always, associated with a temperamental unhappiness so great that, but for the joy which the artist derives from his work, he would be driven to suicide. We cannot, therefore, maintain that even the greatest work may make a man happy, we can only maintain that it must make him less unhappy.

Furthermore, if one is in a profession such as novel writing, where the experience of one's defeats and disappointments may be incorporated and used to give the new work extra dimension or power, so much the greater can its faith-preserving value be. At one level, perhaps the simplest, the writer has the satisfaction of knowing that his wounds haven't incapacitated him forever. At another level, he has the possibly base but nonetheless healing satisfaction of hitting back at those who might have caused his discomforts and at those who have certainly been relishing them. And on a higher plane, if the work is any good at all (and we are talking about a superpro, remember), in using his painful experiences to their best effect he will have to view them with some detachment and in perspective—the prerequisites for fully restored health. It is significant that the disappointments and defeats of just such a man as Fitzgerald, sick but desperately persistent, were central to *The Last Tycoon*—the necessary distancing being effected not only by presenting him as a film producer, Monroe Stahr, rather than as a novelist or even a scriptwriter, but also by basing the character on that of another actual person, Fitzgerald's dead friend Irving Thalberg. Thus Fitzgerald was able to short-circuit any tendency toward self-pity and yet avoid being pushed to the other extreme, equally distorting—that of wry cynicism: a posture he'd resorted to in some of his earlier, more direct attempts to portray his plight, in "The Crack-Up" and other sketches.

One feels that it was with rather similar preservative/creative instincts that two centuries earlier another novelist, also beset with frustrations and debts, seized on a situation that, though superficially very different from his own, and one that had been experienced by another actual person, was essentially the same. So there came to be written *The Life and Strange Surprising Adventures of Robinson Crusoe, of York, Mariner.* In it, Defoe was (to quote Brian Fitzgerald) able to

compensate himself for all the failures of his life—for his bankruptcy, for the degradation of his imprisonment, and the claustrophobic fear of confinement that haunted him ever afterwards

—by becoming the captain of his soul and the master of his fate on an imaginary uninhabited island in the North Atlantic. He could compensate himself for the humiliations he had suffered in public life by doing the actions of government he had never been able to perform in reality, by showing his capacity for ruling and directing and colonizing.

Maxim Gorky called *Robinson Crusoe* "The Bible of the Unconquerable"—but the history of literature is starred with such examples and it would be more properly described as one of the early books in that Bible.

BONUSES

Disappointment and defeat, disease and disaster. . . . They may be regarded as spurs by masochists like Burton and as tests (of fire or acid) by superprofessionals of every kind. And apart from the useful, sometimes vitally necessary character-tempering benefits they bring, when successfully overcome, there are sometimes bonuses. For the golfer Hogan such a bonus came in the form of greatly improved technique, as we have seen in an earlier chapter. For others the bonus may come unnoticed, operating at a far deeper level—the disappointment or defeat serving to clear the ground for more important matters. Writing of Wordsworth's boyhood, De Quincey made the following observation:

In moments of watching for the passage of woodcocks over the hills in moonlight nights, in order that he might snare them, oftentimes the dull gaze of expectation, after it was becoming hopeless, left him liable to effects of mountain scenery under accidents of mighty silence and solitude, which impressed themselves with a depth for which a full tide of success would have allowed no opening.

7

An Eye
for Detail

Horatio Nelson had all the basic power-building qualities
necessary for a successful career as a naval officer: enthusiasm,
single-mindedness, courage. At eighteen he was given his
first command, and by the age of twenty-two he was a post
captain. Admittedly, he lacked the political manipulative
skill that seems to be essential in such a career if the successful progress is to be maintained in peacetime; and in his
early thirties he had to endure a period on half pay and,
much worse, dry land, back on his father's farm. But with the

outbreak of the French Revolution he was once more in his rightful element, in command of a battleship, with his enthusiasm at such a pitch that at times he tended to push his courage beyond the limits that some observers deemed commensurate with his responsibilities. At any rate, it was during this early period of return to active service that he lost his right eye.

By all accounts that didn't do much to cool his courage or dampen his enthusiasm. And one might almost fancy that the single eye helped to narrow and sharpen even further the focus of the single mind. It was certainly an eye for detail. Just as certainly it was this further quality—his passionate attention to the relevant minutiae of his professional tasks—that lifted him above the ruck of other enthusiastic, single-minded, and courageous naval officers and made him the great commander he was.

It was directed onto all phases of his campaigns. Here is an account of the preparations he was continually making during his long Mediterranean chase after the French fleet that was to culminate in the Battle of the Nile:

Every day . . . the men were exercised at their guns and small arms. Whenever the weather permitted the captains went aboard the *Vanguard* to discuss with the admiral the precise function which each was to fulfil in battle. In the "school for captains" on Nelson's quarterdeck they unconsciously entered into his mind till each of his ideas—lucid, precise and devised against every eventuality—became as natural to them as to him. . . .

The keynote of the fleet's readiness for battle was a minute imaginative attention to detail: the sure hallmark of a great leader. "No man," Mahan has written, "was ever better served than Nelson by the inspiration of the hour; no man ever counted less on it." Every ship was ready day and night for action: every man schooled in an exact part. Five thousand wills and bodies moved to a single purpose infinitely diversified in individual function. It was a living discipline which wasted nothing; of muscle, mind or matter. Everything was prepared because everything was foreseen. Thus in the *Alexander* Captain Ball had every spare shroud and sail constantly soaked in water and rolled tight into hard non-inflammable cylinders.*

Before the Battle of Copenhagen, Nelson was to bring this same quality to bear not only in ensuring general preparedness for all eventualities, but also in overcoming a special navigational problem arising from the nature of the tactics he was proposing to adopt: to take his lightest ships with the current up a narrow channel between a shoal known as the Middle Ground and the shore batteries, and then to rejoin the rest of the fleet beyond the shoal without having to turn. To quote Bryant again:

It involved, however, an intricate and dangerous piece of navigation, for the shoal waters round the Middle Ground ran like a mill race, and the fleet had no charts. But Nelson spent the icy, foggy nights of March 30th and 31st in an open boat taking soundings, and he felt confident of his ability to take the battle fleet through the shoals. It was by now his only chance of overcoming the defences.

Such assiduity was maintained during the actions themselves, and it was typical of Nelson that in his last battle, at Trafalgar, after being fatally wounded by a shot that went through his shoulder, lung, and spine, he should spread a handkerchief over his face and the stars on his breast before being carried below to the surgeon—so that the men should not be discouraged by the sight of their commander in chief in such a bad state. And a few hours later, when Hardy went

* From *Nelson* by Sir Arthur Bryant.

down to tell the dying admiral that the battle had been won, one of his first thoughts was to remember the signs of an approaching storm that had been worrying him earlier. "Anchor, Hardy, anchor!" may not have been his last words, but they certainly offer a more significant clue to Nelson's personality and strength than either the maudlin and much-misquoted "Kiss me" (or "Kismet") or the more correct but orotund "God and my country."

Ironically, the shot that killed Nelson came from the deck of the *Redoutable*—a ship with a record that, according to Oliver Warner, "is one of the finest in the history of any navy. She fought two three-deckers, [and] immobilized one of them, the *Victory.* . . . For a 74-gun ship, the feat was brilliant almost beyond belief." And whence the brilliance? Here is an extract from the report of Captain Lucas, her commander:

Ever since the *Redoutable* was fitted out, no measures had been neglected to train the crew in every sort of drill. My ideas were always directed towards fighting by boarding. I so counted upon its success that everything had been prepared to undertake it with advantage. I had had canvas pouches to hold two grenades made for all captains of guns; the cross-belts of these pouches carried a tin tube containing a small match. In all our drills, I made them throw a great number of pasteboard grenades, and I often landed the grenadiers in order to have them explode iron grenades. They had so acquired the habit of hurling them that on the day of battle our topmen were throwing two at a time.

I had 100 carbines fitted with long bayonets on board. The men to whom these were served out were so well accustomed to their use that they climbed half-way up the shrouds to open musketry fire. All those armed with swords were given broad-sword practice every day, and pistols became familiar weapons to them. The grapnels were thrown so skilfully that they would succeed in hooking a ship even though not exactly touching us.

When the drum beat to quarters, each man went to his station fully armed, and with his weapons loaded; he placed them near his gun in nettings nailed between each beam. Finally the crew had themselves such confidence in this manner of fighting that they often urged me to board the first ship with which we should engage.*

Now there are several important points to bear in mind when considering the relationship between attention to detail and the work of superprofessionals like Nelson, and most of them have been touched on in the foregoing examples. There is first the fact that the assiduity was leavened at all times with imagination—the close, practical, sharply focused imagination of a man steeped in the aims and contingencies of his job. It was not the dull, plodding, obsessional assiduity of the slave to detail, the man unable to delegate, or the man who is only too glad to bury his head in massed grains of particularity; and the imagination applied was not the airy, restless, dreamy whimsicality that is too often given the name of imagination. Next there is the fact, linked with the first, that one of the purposes of such close attention to detail is to liberate the mind at the time of action or performance, *and so leave room for inspiration,* for the suddenly proffered advantage deriving from a mistake made by a less well-drilled opponent, or from the too predictable maneuver of an equally assiduous but unimaginative opponent. And then there is the fact that attention to detail of this higher quality is not confined to any one phase of the work—to its execution, say, or planning, or preparation—but that it is maintained throughout. As we shall see, the actual *level* of attention to detail need not be consistent throughout: indeed it had better not be in professions where the execution of the work is narrowly limited in time and subject to pressures beyond

* Quoted by Oliver Warner in *Trafalgar.*

one's control. There must be flexibility, as in the lens of a healthy human eye.

OF MONKS AND MASTERPIECES

All this reminds us that attention to detail as an index of success or excellence should never be confused with that old recipe—much pushed by teachers in previous generations and puritanical communities, and still widely peddled around today—that genius, or talent, or the translation of talent into success, depends on "an infinite capacity for taking pains." Maybe it's the word "pains" that does it, and the suggestion of martyrdom and trial by ordeal, but the advocates of this path rarely hint at any possibility of flexibility or diversion. Flexibility suggests letting up, diversion escape. So, into the collective unconscious of millions of individuals has gone the picture of a long-faced, duly emaciated monk, uncomfortable in his hair shirt and crouched, cushionless in a damp cold cell, over the manuscript he is illuminating. Taking pains, children. A letter a leap year. For the glory of God. Or, since God has been mentioned, the picture might shift to that of the monk's secular cousin, the stone carver, who labors for months (or is it years?) over the head of a mouse in a niche in the bell-tower, a head that might never be seen by another human from one century to the next. But of course God will see it. And the stone carver is exercising his infinite capacity. The inference drawn from this sort of homily was that both monk and carver were geniuses, artists of the highest order, and occasionally a reproduction or photograph would be handed around, depicting certain undoubted masterpieces that must clearly have taken a great deal of time to complete. What were never passed around were any of the multitudinous examples of dull, lifeless, worthless objects on which similar or even greater pains had been lavished.

It was all really a vast pedagogical confidence trick, of which the perpetrators and perpetuators were usually just as much the victims as their charges. It made for easy discipline, for in ordinary circumstances there is nothing the young and eager mind likes better than fussing over details—counting, checking, listing, making the upstrokes light and the down-strokes heavy—with the prospect of high prizes for sheer (and mere) punctiliousness. Only when a child's interest is thoroughly roused does he tend to cut loose, keen to get at the finished product his imagination has presented to his mind's eye, and then, in the pedagogic circumstances described, he would be chided for his lack of pains, slapped down for being slapdash.

Naturally there have been repercussions. The less intelligent, finding that such early attempts at taking pains got them nowhere, have shrugged the whole thing off as a matter of lunacy, of masochism and hermitage, of freaks and mental cripples, of which they want no part. Others, still hankering after glory, have pleaded extenuating circumstances: mute inglorious Miltons citing lack of time, if not lack of the necessary infinity, as the only barrier between them and their undoubted genius. And many of the brighter ones have smelled the rat—that trickster or fool who sold them the idea. For the world of art and entertainment, business and politics, has turned out to be full of examples that seem to give lie to the infinite pains theory. Then the enlightened ones will point to pictures created between breakfast and lunch that, far from being slapdash and worthless, are patently infinitely better than so many of the products over which so much time and sweat have been expended. Geniuses are born, not made, they will tell us. The infinite pains story was a load of garbage. Such critics will, in effect, reverse the figures in that other old kindred recipe: the one about 10 percent inspiration and 90 percent perspiration. So they will veer too far in the opposite direction.

Even the very brightest of the disillusioned are liable to persist in overreacting. Allowing that many masterpieces have indeed had enormous pains lavished on them, they are tempted to take a broad view and put it all down to temperament. Some geniuses need to agonize, others are lucky enough to be able to skip this process. The work comes easy to them. And then of course—the argument might proceed —there are the hampered geniuses: those who really belonged to the latter category who were misguided into behaving like the former, to the detriment of their work generally. Look at Constable, and those famous sketches of subjects that he later worked up into finished full-dress studio paintings, and the universally acknowledged superiority of those sketches.

Let us then look at Constable, though rather more closely than such advocates seem to have done.

First of all, the works in question were not sketches, rapid though their execution may have been. To quote R. H. Wilenski:

They are not sketches in the sense of unfinished pictures or in the sense of shorthand notes for pictures (such as Turner made). Nor are they sketches in the sense of pochades—rapid mechanical notes of purely visual impressions—a type of sketch which Constable also produced in large numbers. They are really *finished pictures* in the sense that they record a conscious experience and record it both completely and without any extraneous additions. Everything in these works—not least the rapid spontaneous deliberately emotive handling—contributes to the true expression of the experience.*

* *English Painting.*

But to make these rapidly executed pictures the great works of art they undoubtedly are required more than luck or inspiration or flair or even sympathy with the scenes depicted. It required a practiced eye and a practiced hand: the eye stored with countless details of the visual effects of sunlight and clouds, wind, rain, dew, mist, on trees and grasses, stones and stumps, and the hand fluent in the numerous methods of translating these effects to the canvas, much as the hand of a writer is able unconsciously to inscribe the words that he feels are necessary for the accurate transference of his thoughts to paper. Indirectly, Constable once associated these visual details of perception and translation with hieroglyphics, when saying: "The art of seeing nature is a thing almost as much to be acquired as the art of reading the Egyptian hieroglyphics"—and of course no one can do that without the closest attention to detail. As Constable himself had pointed out, a few sentences earlier: "If we refer to the lives of all who have distinguished themselves in art or science, we shall find they have always been laborious. The landscape painter must walk in the fields with an humble mind."

And this is precisely what Constable had done most of his life—with the keen-eyed, receptive, wondering humility of the scientist. "Painting," he had declared, in an earlier lecture, "is a science, and should be pursued as an inquiry into the laws of nature. Why, then may not landscape painting be considered as a branch of natural philosophy, of which pictures are but the experiments?" So he took every opportunity to study his material and record his observations in innumerable sketches—the true sketches to which Wilenski refers in the passage quoted—and he was quick to praise anyone who did likewise. ("Claude neglected no mode of study that was calculated to extend his knowledge, and perfect his practice. His evenings were passed at the Academy, and his days in the fields . . .") Constable's intimate friends were well aware of the practice supporting such formal preachings. C. R. Leslie wrote, of a visit to Petworth with the painter:

that as an inmate of the same house, I had an opportunity of witnessing his habits. He rose early, and had often made some beautiful sketch in the park before breakfast. On going into his room one morning, not aware that he had yet been out of it, I found his setting some of these sketches in isinglass. His dressing-table was covered with flowers, feathers of birds, and pieces of bark with lichens and mosses adhering to them, which he had brought home for the sake of their beautiful tints. Mr George Constable [no relation] told me that while on the visit to him, Constable brought from Fittleworth Common, at least a dozen different specimens of sand and earth, of colours from pale to deep yellow, and of light reddish hues to tints almost crimson. The richness of these colours contrasted with the deep greens of the furze and other vegetation on this picturesque heath, delighted him exceedingly, and he carried these earths home carefully preserved in bottles, and also many fragments of the variously coloured stone. In passing with Mr G. Constable some slimy posts near an old mill, he said, "I wish you could cut off, and send their tops to me."*

Another friend wrote:

At all times of the day, at night, and in all seasons of the year, Constable had inexpressible delight in viewing the works of nature. I have been out with him after all colour of the landscape had disappeared, and objects were seen only as skeletons and masses, yet his eye was still active for his art. "These were the

* From C. R. Leslie's *Memoirs of the Life of John Constable Esq., R.A.* this and subsequent quotations concerning Constable have been taken, as well as the extracts from Constable's lectures already quoted.

things," said he, "that Gainsborough studied, and of which we have so many exquisite specimens in his drawings." Constable found undecorated beauties in the nakedness of winter when he lavished admiration on the anatomy of trees, & c. He well knew the *language* of a windmill, and by its expressions could tell you of the winds, and of the skies, and besides this he knew many other tongues that are not written, and are too little studied and understood for the boundless authorities they furnish to artists, to poets, to philosophers, and all true lovers of the wisdom of nature.

Skies were of particular interest to Constable. In a letter to his friend Archdeacon Fisher, he mentions in passing having recently made "about fifty careful studies of skies, tolerably large to be careful." Twenty of these came into the possession of Leslie, who describes them thus:

They are painted in oil, on large sheets of thick paper, and all dated, with the time of day, the direction of the wind, and other memoranda on their backs. On one, for instance, is written, "5th of September, 1822. 10 o' clock, morning, looking south east, brisk wind at west. Very bright and fresh grey clouds running fast over a yellow bed, about half way in the sky."

As will be apparent from various statements in passages already quoted, Constable's passion for the meticulous study of his subject was fierce enough to admit his profiting from the observations of other painters. After all, his subject was not so much nature itself as the depicting of nature and the ways of doing it. So he was not above copying, as an exercise, the schematized studies of cloud formation drawn up by the painter Cozens for the benefit of his pupils: e.g., "streaky clouds at the top of the sky" or "bottom of the sky." Rightly applauding such wholeheartedness, Koestler has said: "By learning to distinguish different types of cloud-formation–

acquiring an articulate cloud-vocabulary as it were—he was able to perceive clouds, and to paint clouds, as nobody had done before."* But such copybook exercises are only the measure of Constable's total commitment—of the superprofessional's true humility in eschewing no possible means of improving his skill. For his studies of skies had a firmer, more organic basis, linked with his upbringing as the son of a miller, and further strengthened by his working in one of his father's mills for about a year after leaving school. After quoting Constable's younger brother, Abram ("When I look at a mill painted by John, I feel that it will *go round,* which is not always the case with those by other artists"), Leslie notes that: "By a wind-miller every change of the sky is watched with peculiar interest; and it will appear from Constable's description of this plate [an engraving of one of his early sketches, *Spring*] that the time spent as one, was not wholly lost to him as a painter." Here is that description:

It may perhaps give some idea of one of those bright and silvery days in the spring, when at noon large garish clouds surcharged with hail or sleet sweep with their broad shadows the fields, woods, and hills; and by their depths enhance the value of the vivid greens and yellows so peculiar to the season. The *natural history,* if the expression may be used, of the skies, which are so particularly marked in the hail squalls at this time of the year, is this:– The clouds accumulate in very large masses, and from their loftiness seem to move but slowly: immediately upon these large clouds appear numerous opaque patches, which are only small clouds passing rapidly before them, and consisting of isolated portions detached probably from the larger cloud. These floating much nearer the earth may perhaps fall in with a stronger current of wind, which as well as their comparative lightness causes them to move with greater rapidity; hence they

* From *The Act of Creation.*

are called by wind-millers and sailors, *messengers,* and always portend bad weather. They float midway in what may be termed the lanes of the clouds; and from being so situated, are almost uniformly in shadow, receiving a reflected light only, from the clear blue sky immediately above them. In passing over the bright parts of the large clouds they appear as darks; but in passing the shadowed parts, they assume a grey, a pale, or a lurid hue.

Such then was the meticulous attention to detail that enabled Constable to produce his rapid "painless" master-pieces—an attention to detail bestowed not nearly so much in execution as in that aspect of a superprofessional's work so rarely touched upon: his continuous close and usually life-long background interest in his specialty.

PREPARING THE GROUND

In the life of any professional there arise against such a back-ground of continuous interest the tasks themselves: the books to be written, the concertos to be performed, the pictures to be painted, the battles to be fought, the races to be run, the songs to be recorded, the games to be played, the fish to be caught, the safes to be rifled, the thieves to be trapped, the cases to be contested, the cases to be judged, the criminals to be rehabilitated, the sinners to be saved, the plays to be produced, the deals to be swung, the geese to be cooked, the gardens to be created, the barns to be converted, the heathen to be converted, the concertos to be written, the pictures to be sold, the pictures to be bought, the races to be reported, the songs to be marketed, the growths to be removed, the patients to be nursed . . . and so on. And no matter what the profession, each task has three distinct phases: the planning, the preparation, and the execution. Naturally, the conscious attention to detail given to each phase will vary in intensity according to the nature of the task. As we have already noted in tasks involving strong and persistent outside pressures beyond one's direct control, and those with stringent time limits, it will go better with the participant if the details have been thoroughly assimilated beforehand. For example, a boxer will be given little time for the sort of conscious detailed analysis of an opponent's moves afforded to a chess player; just as a sprinter's conscious attention to detail must be suspended with the crack of the starting pistol, whereas with a long-distance runner it must continue to be maintained throughout the race at least at the level reached during the earlier phases. This question of emphasis in relation to the nature of the work and the amount of attention to be paid to detail is one that the superprofessional, or the aspirant, has to come to terms with early in his career. Nevertheless, two common factors seem to emerge when considering the field as a whole. One is that in all professions the amount of attention to detail paid *generally*—the mulling and musing and browsing arising from sustained interest in one's subject—the background element—helps significantly to determine the quality of an individual's performance. And the other common factor is that no matter how little attention to detail is considered necessary in the other phases, to neglect it in the preparatory stage is not only to incur great risks unnecessarily but also to throw away the possibility of obtaining substantial bonuses.

As we have seen, time and again during the course of this investigation, a sustained background interest in the details of one's profession, no matter how haphazard the gathering, nor how unconsidered the trifles picked up, can help enormously in dealing with mistakes or deficiencies in one's performance and in facing and overcoming setbacks. It facilitates the tracing of precedents and so the preparation of correctives. It forewarns one of the accidents and disasters that can happen to the best and so prepares the individual for the shocks that are almost inevitably in store for his own system and susceptibilities. It is in fact a low-keyed form of pre-preparation, and it is with particular regard to this conditioning, psychological aspect that I propose to examine the preparatory phase itself.

In a sense, preparation *is* attention to detail. The broad outlines of policy or strategy having been laid down in the planning stage, the time arrives for getting down to brass tacks: the logistics, the soundings, the testing, the sampling, the exercises, the rehearsals, the practice of specific actions, the reconnaissances, the consultations with specialists, the gathering of spares or reserves, and more and still more practice in the light of relevant information about one's opponent or the conditions likely to be encountered. As was noted in relation to Nelson and Lucas and their strength in this respect, the more thorough and intelligent the preparations, the greater the confidence that is generated and transmitted; while the less there has been left to chance as a negative threatening element, the more alert one's faculties are for seizing any positive opportunity it may present. These are the more obvious psychophysiological bonuses to be picked up at this stage. But there are also others, of even greater value, touching the springs of creativity itself, which begin to emerge when a wide enough variety of examples is studied.

Let us start with Brunel again. In some ways, his becomes a cautionary and, in the end, a tragic tale. Already, in connection with other aspects of the subject, we have noted how his meticulousness stood him in good stead in times of stress; in his last turbulent years it was to become a literally vital factor. But here we find him in his prime, temporarily untroubled by any major setback or disaster, involved completely in the construction of a railroad:

At this period Brunel kept what might be called a common-place book in which he collected any material which was likely to be of use to him in building the railway. This has survived as an example of his thoroughness and of his astonishing mastery of all the infinite detail involved in railway construction, including as it does a list of the species of grasses most suitable for growing in different soils for the purpose of consolidating new earthworks and tables of rainfall figures and local times for places along the route. Here, amongst much fascinating information of the most diverse description we find a note to the effect that whereas the original cast-iron rails laid on the Hetton Colliery Railway had a life of from ten to twelve years, the malleable iron rails laid by the manager, Luke Dunn, in November 1831 between Hunter's Lane Engine House and the fourth incline had a life of only four years.*

That falls somewhere between the pre-preparatory general-gleaning aspect and the preparatory stage proper. But here is Brunel in full spate, instructing an assistant on a project that was the great engineer's answer to the Army Medical Service's problems in the Crimea: a complete, transportable, speedily erectable hospital. (An answer that arrived too late to be of much use, incidentally, thanks to the dilatoriness of the authorities, who tended to regard him, civilian and part foreigner that he was, with something of the suspicion they had for the woman Nightingale.)

All plans will be sent in duplicate. . . . By steamer *Hawk* or *Gertrude* I shall send a derrick and most of the tools, and as each vessel sails you shall hear by post what is in her. . . .

The son of the contractor goes with the head foreman, ten carpenters, the foreman of the W. C. makers and two men who worked on the iron houses and can lay pipes. I am sending a

---

* From L. T. C. Rolt's biography of Brunel, as are the other quotations concerning the engineer.

small forge and two carpenter's benches, but you will need assistant carpenters and labourers, fifty to sixty in all. . . . Do not *let anything induce you to alter the general system and arrangement that I have laid down.*

A few days later he has an afterthought:

I would only add to my instructions attention to closet floors by paving or other means so that water cannot lodge in it but it can be kept perfectly clean.

A subject that he takes up with the doctor in charge:

. . . I obtained authority yesterday to purchase one third of the required quantity of bedding and some other similar stores and they are now going aboard with the buildings. I have added twenty shower baths, one for each ward and six vapour baths. You will be amazed to find also certain boxes of paper for the water closets—I find that at a cost of a few shillings per day an ample supply could be furnished and the mechanical success of the W. C.s will be much influenced by this. I hope you will succeed in getting it used and not abused. In order to assist in this important object I send out some printed notices or handbills to be stuck up . . . in the closet room opposite each closet exhorting the men to use the apparatus properly and telling them how to do so. If you do not approve of such appeals the paper can be used for other purposes and perhaps impart some information in its exit from this upper world.

It is doubly sad that this brilliant, thoughtful, and imaginatively meticulous man should end his career contractually bound in his most ambitious project—the construction of his ship *The Great Eastern*—to a shipbuilder who was both slipshod and dishonest. This was the smooth-talking Scott Russell, and it may be argued that Brunel's close and constant attention to detail should have been extended to the personal qualities of possible associates. At any rate, the resultant conflicts and frustrations, coupled with the extra burden of work imposed by the need to make up for the other man's deficiencies, fatally undermined Brunel's health. Only his determination kept him going through the final humiliating period, when Russell's strategic bankruptcy compelled Brunel to hurry the launch. "Otherwise," his son was to write, "I.K.B. would not have started on 3 November when none of the tackle had been properly tested . . ." That launch miscarried, and only after several more agonizing attempts was the ship finally afloat, at the end of the following January. By then Brunel's health was completely broken, and though he lived for another twenty months or so, he never recovered. The final blow came on hearing in his sickroom that there had been a disastrous explosion on one of the finally fitted ship's trials—an accident due largely to an oversight in the routine checking job for which Russell had been responsible. The ship survived, thanks to the engineering skill that Brunel had put into the design; but her creator was dead before nightfall.

Now there are two points to note here, before passing on to the next examples. The first is that no matter how big the project or how numerous the people involved, the close attention to detail at this stage must emanate from the man in charge if it is to have its maximum value. One feels that it would have been much less use, for instance, for Brunel to have said to his undoubtedly competent assistants, "Here are my plans for the hospital. Work out the details for yourselves." There has to be orchestration and, more important, there has to be the opportunity for details to germinate and cluster, to link up and proliferate, and the likeliest plot for such subsequent growth is in the mind that first took them in. In short, the *attention* becomes the key word: the attention of a loving parent or skillful gardener. When Brunel insists that his assistants let nothing induce them to alter the *general* system, etc., one suspects (and the context bears out the suspicion) that it is also the *particulars* he doesn't want them to dismiss or neglect. The second point is really a corollary of the first. A man of such genius may delegate or enter into partnership—indeed, he will probably have no choice as his career develops—but these arrangements should be so made that he has at all times direct access to and potential ultimate control over the smallest details of a project. Besides the fact that his is the creative genius and these might be seeds of vast importance, there is the high probability that, steeped in the business as he is, he is the one best equipped to realize the significance of a hairline crack or a missing bolt.

In much the same case is the public performer or interpretative artist who has to rely on the skills of others when presenting his finished performance. One of the most obvious examples—almost an archetype of the category—is the orchestra conductor. Great though the individual skills of the players under him may be, and adept at playing together though the complete orchestra sometimes prides itself in being, the conductor will never, if he is good at his job, neglect the details. Thus Barbirolli would spend hours on the scores "bowing" the master copies for the strings, often working through the nights after spending the days on the "constant and detailed rehearsing" that he knew to be essential if an orchestra was to reach the heights. And, as with the scoremarking, the attention to detail went beyond and behind the rehearsals themselves, to be focused on the abilities of individual players—into the teaching as well as the interpretative aspect. When asked about the possible dictatorial element in all this, he replied:

There can be no great orchestra, with a *style* of its own, without a head of great quality, both as a teacher and as an interpreter, and by style I mean not only a particular characteristic but a suppleness and variety of style that can attune itself to music of all kinds and periods. . . . The Hallé are even taught to play with different kinds of vibrato, for different kinds of music (every 1st class player should be equipped with this quality). There are, of course, different types of portamentos, though few are aware of these, and there is the important question also of *no vibrato* and *no portamento,* which in any case must be used only to stress certain melodic and emotional elements, as Mahler well knew.

In widely differing fields, the same meticulousness has to be shown by any solo performer who depends for his material on the work of a team. For example, three or four writers are employed on the six-minute monologue spot with which Johnny Carson opens his television show five nights a week. Each of them gets to work at 10.30 A.M. and, in the words of Bill Majeski:

You sit in your office and start going through your largest source of material—newspapers and magazines. You study The New York Times, The Daily News, The Wall Street Journal, The Washington Post, The New York Post, Womens Wear Daily, Life, Time, Newsweek and other lesser-known publications . . .

Your quarry in this daily scanning is anything unusual and/or topical. ("Teachers in Newark are striking for higher pay. They need it. They have to pay for their own bullets.")*

By the middle of the afternoon, each writer will have come up with twelve to fifteen jokes, and these are submitted to Carson by the head writer. Thus:

Carson, alone in his office, reads anywhere from 40 to 60 jokes daily and chooses maybe a dozen. He checks the ones he likes,

* From an article in *The New York Times,* 1 August 1971.

numbers them and underlines the key words to be printed on the cue cards.

This includes the selection of "savers," backup jokes to be used in case a gag should die, usually making reference (carefully unbarbed) to the slowness of the audience. (E.g., "SAVER—This is the type of crowd that would send an Arrow shirt to General Custer.") Nor does Carson leave much to chance in the main part of the program, when interviewing the guests. Although relying mainly on his own wit for his comments at that stage, he makes sure that he has a battery of "ad libs" concocted by his writers at a late-afternoon meeting—just in case. ("As an example, an Oriental karate team appeared recently and the interview notes said: 'Dr. U will break a cinder block with his head.' Bradford the head writer looks around for comment. Someone grunts, 'Better U than me.' Bradford nods, types it on a card, presses a buzzer and secretary Alison Mills appears, whisks it off to Carson and another ad-lib is born.")

Majeski doesn't mention anything about the star's punctiliousness beyond the limits of the written material, but it would be very surprising if it were to end there. A public performance involves much more than the words to be spoken or the notes to be played. Such imponderables as expression, style, and timing have an immensely important part to play, and these in turn can be affected not only by such other imponderables as the mood of an audience,* but also by definite measurable factors, often quite trivial in themselves. The temperature, the humidity, the lighting, smells, noises—all can have an effect, adverse or otherwise,

---

* A young advertising agency executive once complained bitterly to me that when the show was headquartered in New York, Carson was very strict about the issue of free tickets to agency people, saying he was reluctant to have in the audience large numbers of smart-assed sophisticates sitting on their hands instead of applauding.

on both performer and audience. Here is Carl Flesch, writing in his monumental *The Art of Violin Playing,* on the subject of what he calls "hindrances . . . to the realization of our artistic intentions during our activities before the public":

Spatial Hindrances

Hereby we understand hindrances outside the radius of the player's person and of his instrument, and which are called forth by certain peculiarities of the space surrounding him, above all, of the *concert platform.* It is hard to imagine the number of circumstances operating unfavorably which originate in this apparently most insignificant component of the concert hall. There is the *"freshly scrubbed"* platform which, especially in little provincial towns, has been thoroughly washed with soap and water before the concert, in honor of the event. In the evening the evaporating moisture, favored by the heated temperature of the concert hall, develops invisible clouds of steam, which envelop the instrument and the strings, make the latter's tone seem veiled, and put both strings and artist out of tune. *Creaking* noises of the platform, usually a result of the use of wood not sufficiently seasoned, belongs in the category of acoustic hindrances. They seem preferably to accompany accented bow-strokes, in which the more strenuous movements of the body weigh more heavily on the platform. Here the danger exists that instinctive fear of these disturbing noises may limit the activity of the right arm, under which again, the power of expression as a whole will suffer. The copious *floral* decorations too, so often arranged on the platform on jubilee celebrations of famous composers or conductors, to enhance the festal spirit, increase the humidity of the air and also exert an unfavorable influence. When the platform *slopes* too much, as is the case with most theatre stages, the player leans too far forward and is in danger of losing his balance. (*Ole Bull* is said always to have played in heelless shoes for this reason.) The platform may also be too *high,* something which may be fatal to the player inclined to giddiness or agoraphobia, and who feels he is standing on the edge of an abyss.

Lack of space on the platform, especially when the artist is playing with an orchestra, can indispose an artist for the entire evening. He has agoraphobia in every direction. Too close to the concertmaster's desk, he is afraid of knocking against it. Besides, the first violins are playing all too close to him. If he steps back a little too far, he gets in the way of the conductor's baton, while immediately before his feet there yawns an abyss. And woe to him if, in addition to such space-limitations, he has . . . a "long range" conductor as an accompanist, one who thinks no beat gets its full value unless it be more than a yard long. The collisions which unavoidably result under such circumstances have already permanently damaged many instruments and friendships. Here, too, should be mentioned the sight, at bottom a gratifying one, of a platform on which a circle of auditors surrounds the player. In addition to all the drawbacks already mentioned, the artist must also suffer from the reaction of the listeners, who personally radiate a warmth as ardent as their enthusiasm. If he has his performance at all in mind the player will ruthlessly clear the way, and get sufficient room for his movements before beginning.

Now as to the *temperature* of the surrounding space. The thermometer should never exceed 20–24 degrees Celsius (approximately 65–69 degrees Fahrenheit). In halls that are too *cold,* the instrument will not "speak" well, the fingers do not get warm enough, the finger-tips remain hard and inelastic, and the bow-hairs are too tensed. When the temperature is too *high,* we have increased perspiration, the strings get out of tune, the tone sounds veiled, the fingers slip on the fingerboard and the strings as though on a saponaceous substratum, and the sureness of the whole hand is noticeably diminished. Only the experience of years will familiarize the artist with the defensive measures he must apply in such cases. Above all, a few hours before the concert, he should try *personally* to investigate the temperature conditions of the hall. He will then still have time enough to alter them in the one or the other respect. Conformity between the temperature of the artist's room (at the concert hall), and that of the hall itself is also very important. For, of course, the tem-

it also suggests an *unnecessary or unreasonable excessiveness.*
Is the true virtuoso really likely to be thrown by an un-
friendly face in the second row? Will his performance be
significantly marred by too strong an odor of chrysanthe-
mums? Almost certainly not. But the anticipation and elimination of such possibilities are bound to help in freeing the
mind for more important matters during the performance (as
with Nelson and his captains and crews), and, over and above
this, the whole process might well help to generate a positive
spiritual influence, something more than the sum total of
physical and psychological advantages secured. In other words,
far from being *bogged down* by details, as the popular expression has it, the superprofessional can actually derive from
them, when intelligently amassed, a *buoyancy.*

In a very different context we find this transcendental
power of attention to detail at work in Thomas Mann's character Felix Krull. Here, the young confidence man (who is
also meant to be regarded as an artist) describes his feelings
on entering the room for a military physical examination.
Determined to fail, and so evade compulsory service, he has
gone to endless trouble to discover and rehearse the symp-
toms of a chronic sickness with which he hopes to fool the
doctor and the board.

At such moments one is blind, and it was only in blurred
outline that the scene penetrated to my at once excited and
bemused consciousness . . . To the left of the table stood the
doctor, he too very shadowy in my eyes, especially since he had
the window at his back. I, however, inwardly repelled by so many
importunate glances turned on me, bemused by the dream-like
sensation of being in a highly vulnerable and defenceless position, seemed to myself to be alone, cut off from every relationship, nameless, ageless, floating free and pure in empty space, a
sensation I have preserved in memory as not only not disagree-

able but actually precious. The fibres of my body might continue to quiver, my pulse go on beating wildly and irregularly; nevertheless, from then on, my spirit, if not sober, was yet completely calm, and what I said and did in the sequel happened as though without my co-operation and in the most natural fashion—indeed, to my own momentary amazement. Here exactly lies the value of long advance preparation and conscientious immersion in what is to come: at the critical moment something somnambulistic occurs, half-way between action and accident, doing and being dealt with, which scarcely requires our attention, all the less so because the demands actuality makes on us are usually lighter than we expected, and we find ourselves, so to speak, in the situation of a man who goes into battle armed to the teeth only to discover that the adroit use of a single weapon is all he needs for victory. To protect himself the more readily in minor contingencies the prudent man practises what is most difficult, and he is happy if he needs only the most delicate and subtle weapons in order to triumph, as he is naturally averse to anything gross and crude and accommodates himself to their use only in cases of necessity.*

With this passage, and its suggestion of an incantatory, self-hypnotic effect of ultradetailed preparation, we are now drawing close to one of the most important elements of creativity: the link between the amassing of concrete detail and the working of the subconscious mind. In the examples already discussed we have been considering the matter in relation to painters, naval commanders, engineers, musicians, entertainers, and confidence tricksters, and some of the ways in which a saturation of detail can help greatly to facilitate particular tasks in hand. But there seems to be also a creative function in the operation of this link—as if the details sometimes act as grains of gunpowder to produce flashes of intuition—and nowhere is this aspect more strikingly evident

* *Confessions of Felix Krull, Confidence Man.*

than in the field of scientific discovery. Here, once again, is Koestler on Kepler:

We saw him plod, with infinite patience, along dreary stretches of trial-and-error procedure, then suddenly become airborne when a lucky guess or hazard presented him with an opportunity. What enabled him to recognize instantly his chance when the number 0.00429 turned up in an unexpected context was the fact that not only his waking mind, but his sleepwalking unconscious self was saturated with every conceivable aspect of his problem, not only with the numerical data and ratios, but also with an intuitive "feel" of the physical forces, and of the *Gestalt* configurations which it involved.

Once again we find the "sleepwalking" image and, far from being a romantic sport, an element to be found only in the early rough-and-tumble days of modern science, the same process can still be found busily at work in these supposedly more coldly objective, more highly systematized, more "scientific" times. What is more, despite this increasingly rigorous and strenuously unemotional context—probably because of it—the sudden intuitive connection is often indirect, with the facts gathered in dealing with one problem suddenly producing the solution to quite another. In comparatively recent years one of the most striking mutiple instances of this was provided by Pasteur who, as Koestler reminds us, once stated that "Fortune favors the prepared mind." Now we have already seen the truth of this demonstrated sufficiently clearly in Nelson's case, but here it is given a startling twist, as if the great admiral's preparations for Trafalgar had contributed *directly* to the victory at Waterloo, or had put him in the way of inventing the nuclear submarine. For Pasteur's speculations about the asymmetry of molecules proved so intoxicating to the great biologist that, in Koestler's words, they caused him to embark on a series of fantastic experiments, aiming at nothing less than the creation of life by means of imitating the asymmetric action of nature in the laboratory, using powerful magnets and all kinds of optical tricks.*

Almost the classical mad scientist of the "chiller theatres" and "creature features" of the movie and television screen, one might think. Fortunately for humanity, however, another cliché of romantic drama intervened. The Great Scientist Had To Eat. So, occasionally, Pasteur earned his bread and butter by accepting commissions to inquire into such comparatively trivial matters as an epidemic disease among silkworms, the keeping qualities of wine and beer, the turning of beet sugar into alcohol, and of course the souring of milk. Being the man he was, he entered into these investigations with great thoroughness and zest, even with patriotic and local fervor—as in the case of the beet-sugar problem, which involved one of the main industries of the region of France in which he worked. But the zest and thoroughness paid unexpected dividends. Koestler again:

In examining the fermented juice of the beet, he found in it a component, amyl alcohol, which turned out to be optically active. Therefore its molecules must be asymmetrical; but according to the grand design [which Pasteur had been exploring in the private experiments already mentioned], asymmetry is the privilege and secret of life; therefore fermentation came from the activity of living things, of microbes. At this point the chain reaction set in which fused the germ theory of fermentation to the germ theory of disease. Thus did the alchemist's pipe-dream give birth to modern medicine—as Kepler's chimerical quest for the harmonies [of the spheres] led to modern astronomy.

* In *The Act of Creation*, in which Koestler examines, in fascinating detail, the whole question of what he has termed "bisociation" in the fields of art and science.

Similarly, Pasteur's investigations into the disorders to which beer is liable led, through study of the main fermentation processes and the conditions of deterioration, to the discovery of microorganisms; the silkworm investigations, to the confirmation that contagious diseases are formed by microbes; and thence to the principles of sterilization, pasteurization, immunization, antisepsis, and so on. Without the grand synthesizing dream, quixotic though it might have appeared, the various affinities leading to these discoveries would probably never have been noticed. But equally it may be claimed that without the supersaturation of detail introduced by the "trivial" investigations the dream itself would probably have become sterile, and its intuitions fruitless.

So far we have been dealing with details in the mass, as it were. But attention to detail can mean just that—attention to the single detail—and where the singleness is coupled with singularity, and the stubbornness with which it resists a satisfactory explanation is matched by the persistence of the mind attending to it, the result can be a discovery as epoch-making as any deriving from the saturation process. Indeed, as Jacques Nicolle has pointed out in his study of Pasteur,* the first links in that scientist's chain of discoveries had in them much of this direct single-combat quality—with (1) the scientist, still a young student, reading an account by the celebrated chemist Mitscherlich of the apparently illogical behavior of two sets of crystals; (2) being profoundly dissatisfied with this account; and (3) two years later going on to conduct a series of experiments that didn't end until he had resolved the troublesome contradiction (and in the process deduced the theory of molecular disymmetry).

An equally striking example is furnished by Freud. Here was a scientific worker who could be very impatient of the

* *Louis Pasteur: A Master of Scientific Inquiry.*

drudgery involved in amassing details to support an insight once made, and whose attention to detail in everyday affairs seemed to consist in cutting down to the minimum the number of details to be attended to. "Thus," (to quote Ernest Jones) "he would own no more than three suits of clothes, three pairs of shoes, and three sets of underclothing. Packing, even for a long holiday, was a very simple matter." Nevertheless,

his great strength, though sometimes also his weakness, was the quite extraordinary respect he had for *singular fact*. This is surely a very rare quality. In scientific work people continually dismiss a single observation when it does not appear to have any connection with other data or general knowledge. Not so Freud. The single fact would fascinate him, and he could not dismiss it from his mind until he had found some explanation of it. The practical value of this mental quality depends on another one: judgement. The fact in question may be really insignificant and the explanation of it of no interest; that way lies crankiness. But it may be a previously hidden jewel or a speck of gold that indicates a vein of ore. Psychology cannot yet explain on what the flair or intuition depends that guides the observer to follow up something his feelings tell him is important, not as a thing in itself, but as an example of some wide law of nature.*

Again we find the note of interdependence being struck. Without the transcendent quality—the flair, the knack, the talent, the gift—the significant detail will probably be overlooked or, if spotted, dismissed. Yet without the more mundane mechanical ability and willingness to attend to detail, to sift through masses of them patiently (for Freud could certainly be assiduous enough in the questing, stalking phases of his work, no matter how cavalier he may have been after

* From *The Life and Work of Sigmund Freud.*

the quarry had been captured), the gift would be of small value.

DETAIL AS A CORRECTIVE

As I have suggested earlier, intuitions are not always necessarily fruitful. The knowledge gained (to paraphrase Webster) "without rational thought and inference" can be misleading or useless. And where this proves to be the case, or where the spark refuses to jump at all, a return to plodding painstaking analysis can be successful—as Stanislavski found in the following instance, when studying the part of an old man.

The hardest thing for me . . . was the speech of old age. I did not guess it intuitively and was forced to seek it by artificial means, technical means, and the methods of creating the pronunciation of age.

First of all I turned to the old man that served me as a model and looked in his mouth to see what happened there when he removed his upper plate of artificial teeth. Between the lower teeth and the upper gum there is formed a crack. I tried to make exactly such a crack between my upper and lower teeth. In order to do this I had to move my lower jaw forward. This made me lisp and interfered with my speech. Nevertheless, having created this obstacle, I did not try to make it greater, but tried to speak as clearly as possible and to pronounce every letter. In order to do this I was forced to pay more attention to my speech and to speak more slowly than was my wont. There appeared a slow rhythm of speech and this reminded me of a very old man whose state I guessed emotionally.*

In other words, intuition was courted, coaxed, and eventually conjured after all, by a review of detail after sharply focused detail.

---

* From *My Life in Art.*

Similarly, where the "intuition" is spurious—merely a strong inclination derived from prejudice, bias presented as deep conviction—attention to detail may be a powerful test and corrective, as Machiavelli was quick to perceive. He began by examining a situation that arose in Ancient Rome when the people became restive about the consulate, demanding that either the office be thrown open to plebeians or the consuls' authority reduced. To counter this, the nobles suggested a compromise: the appointment of four tribunes with consular power—these tribunes to be either plebeians or nobles. Since this offered them a share in the highest office, the plebs were satisfied. But, Machiavelli interjects, "An event now took place which is noteworthy." The people went on to elect four nobles.

Now in Livy's opinion this demonstrated two things: (a) the change that takes place in men's attitudes once a struggle is concluded, leaving room for "unbiased judgment"; and (b) the "modesty, fairness and highmindedness" of the people concerned in that event. Machiavelli digs deeper.

If one asks how this could have come about, I believe it came about because men make quite a number of mistakes about things in general, but not so many about particulars. In general the Roman plebs thought that they deserved the consulate because they were the more numerous party in the city, because it was they who had been exposed to greater danger in the wars, because it was they who by brawn and muscle had kept Rome free and made it powerful. . . . But when it came to deciding which particular members of their party to elect, they recognized their weakness and judged that no one of them was worthy of that of which all of them, taken together, had seemed to be worthy. . . .

He then goes on to back this with two further instances. The first concerned the situation in Capua just after the Romans had been routed by Hannibal at Cannae, and the populace were thirsting for the blood of the senate and quite prepared to turn the city over to the Carthaginians. This was forestalled by the chief magistrate, Pacuvius Calavius, who reconciled the plebs to the nobility by a stratagem that must have warmed Machiavelli's heart. Warning the senate of the grave danger they and the city were in, Pacuvius persuaded the senators to let him lock them up and, in a way that would open the path to reconciliation, "appeal to the power that the populace would thus have of chastising them." Then

he called a meeting of the populace, and told them that the time had come when they could humble the pride of the nobility and obtain vengeance for the injuries done them. . . . He was sure, however, that they would not want their city to remain without a government, so that, if they proposed to kill the old senators, it would be necessary to appoint new ones. With this end in view he had put the names of all the senators in a bag, from which he would proceed to draw them in their presence. He would then put to death those whose names had been drawn, one after the other, as soon as they had found for each a successor. He then began by drawing out one name. On hearing the man's name an uproar was raised, and they called him a proud and cruel and arrogant fellow. Pacuvius then called on them to appoint someone in his stead; whereupon the shouting subsided altogether, and after a pause one of the plebs was nominated. At his name some began to hiss, some to laugh, some to abuse him in one way, some in another. And so it went on, time upon time, till all who had been nominated had been judged to be unworthy of senatorial rank.

Thus, as Machiavelli points out, "the mistake they had been making was discovered as soon as they were forced to get down to particulars."

Finally, moving closer to his own time, he cites the unrest in Florence after the expulsion of the princes in 1494—with members of the popular party grumbling at the anarchy and corruptness that ensued. For this they blamed the citizens who had fomented the disturbances, saying that they had done so simply to take advantage of the troubles and promote their own kind of state, and the grumblers threatened "that if ever they got into the Signoria they would show them their mistake and would chastise them."

One can almost see Machiavelli shaking his head and smiling thinly at this, as he goes on to write:

It has often happened that a man of this sort has risen to the highest office, and, when he has got there, has looked at things more closely and so has come to recognize the source of the disorders, the dangers which they entail, and the difficulty of putting matters right. Realizing that it is circumstances, not men, that have brought the disorders about, he has then quickly changed both his mind and his line of conduct; for acquaintance with things in detail has removed the wrong impression that had been taken for granted when only general considerations were taken into account.

Another example of the way detail can act as a corrective lens when the imagination tends to run out of control is offered in the following extract from Robert Louis Stevenson's essay on "The Art of Writing:"

It is, perhaps, not often that a map figures so largely in a tale, yet it is always important. The author must know his countryside, whether real or imaginary, like his hand; the distances, the points of the compass, the place of the sun's rising, the behaviour of the moon, should all be beyond cavil. And how troublesome the moon is! I have come to grief over the moon in *Prince Otto,* and so soon as that was pointed out to me, adopted a precaution which I recommend to other men—I never write now without an almanack. With an almanack, and the map of the country, and the plan of every house, either actually plotted on paper or already and immediately apprehended in the mind, a man may hope to avoid some of the grossest possible blunders. With a map before him, he will scarce allow the sun to set in the east, as it does in *The Antiquary*. With the almanack at hand, he will scarce allow two horsemen, journeying on the most urgent affair, to employ six days, from three of the Monday morning till late in the Saturday night, upon a journey of, say, ninety or a hundred miles, and before the week is out, and still on the same nags, to cover fifty in one day, as may be read at length in the inimitable novel of *Rob Roy*. And it is certainly well, though far from necessary, to avoid such "croppers". But it is my contention —my superstition, if you like—that who is faithful to his map, and consults it, and draws from it his inspiration, daily and hourly, gains positive support, and not mere negative immunity from accident. The tale has a root there; it grows in that soil; it has a spine of its own behind the words. Better if the country be real, and he has walked every foot of it and knows every milestone. But even with imaginary places, he will do well in the beginning to provide a map; as he studies it, relations will appear that he had not thought upon; he will discover obvious, though unsuspected, shortcuts and footprints for his messengers; and even when a map is not all the plot, as it was in *Treasure Island*, it will be found to be a mine of suggestion.

So, yet again, we see the interdependence at work—this time all the more clearly for being manifested on the surface, in full consciousness—with the details not only correcting but suggesting and molding new sounder imaginative developments.

But with Machiavelli and the errors to which the public imagination is susceptible we had already gone beyond the preparatory stages of highly specialized projects and into a much wider field, where we are presented with a new question: Which of the qualities discussed in this study are the most profitably and readily applicable to everyday life? Those teachers and other would-be improvers who lean heavily on the illustrious example would probably say all or most.

Others, remembering the tremendously important part that the obsessive, success-hungry element usually plays in providing the power that activates those qualities, might hesitate to name any. For instance, at first sight attention to detail itself would appear to be the most obvious candidate for such a transference. Dickens certainly thought so.

The one safe, serviceable, certain, remunerative, attainable quality in every study and in every pursuit is the quality of attention. My own invention or imagination such as it is . . . would never have served me as it has, but for the habit of commonplace, humble, patient, daily, toiling, drudging attention. . . . Like certain plants which the poorest peasant may grow in the poorest soil, it can be cultivated by anyone and it is certain in its own good season to bring forth flowers and fruit.*

Goethe, on the other hand, had his doubts—as he makes evident in his lampoon on the pedantic type:

> *Thanks to my diligence, my wisdom is growing—*
> *If I but persevere I shall be all-knowing.*

It is a difference of opinion we shall be examining in the next and final chapter.

---

* From an address given to the Birmingham and Midland Institution, quoted by Una Pope-Hennessy in *Charles Dickens.*

8

Everyday Excellence?

The transition isn't easy, even for the superprofessionals themselves, even when applying the more superficial elements of their working habits to everyday life. Thus there is something parabolic about Edith Wharton's amusing account of the incident occurring on a car journey with Henry James, when their chauffeur lost his way and the Master took it upon himself to inquire directions of an elderly passer-by.

"My good man, if you will be good enough to come here, please; a little nearer—so," and as the old man came up: "My friend, to put it to you in two words, this lady and I have just arrived here from *Slough;* that is to say, to be more strictly accurate, we have recently *passed through* Slough on our way here, having actually motored to Windsor from Rye, which was our point of departure; and the darkness having overtaken us, we should be much obliged if you would tell us where we are now in relation, say, to the High Street, which, as you of course know, leads to the Castle, after leaving on the left hand the turn down to the railway station."

I was not surprised to have this extraordinary appeal met by silence, and a dazed expression on the old wrinkled face at the window; nor to have James go on: "In short" (his invariable prelude to a fresh series of explanatory ramifications), "in short, my good man, what I want to put to you in a word is this: supposing we have already (as I have reason to think we have) driven past the turn down to the railway station (which, in that case, by the way, would probably not have been on our left hand, but on our right), where are we now in relation to . . ."

"Oh, please," I interrupted, feeling myself utterly unable to sit through another parenthesis, "do ask him where the King's Road is."

"Ah—? The King's Road? Just so! Quite right! Can you, as a matter of fact, my good man, tell us where in relation to our present position the King's Road exactly *is?*"

"Ye're in it," said the aged face at the window.*

Here we have the application of a comparatively minor feature of a great man's work (his style) to a comparatively minor problem of daily life. No doubt, too, the anecdote has been somewhat colored in the telling, even as it was probably quite consciously touched up in the enactment. Nevertheless, the moral is clear and true and serious enough: that the methods applicable to the professional field, and the qualities that make for success there, are not readily negotiable outside

---

* From *A Backward Glance* by Edith Wharton.

it. That the superprofessionals themselves find this to be so is clearly evident from the messes and scrapes so many of them find themselves in from time to time: the broken marriages, the bankruptcies, the disaffected children, the alcoholism, the general muddle. Men and women who have learned to come to terms with their professional deficiencies—to eradicate them or even use them constructively—fail to do the slightest positive thing to help put right their more obvious and comparatively more easily rectifiable faults as husbands, wives, lovers, parents, landlords, tenants, drivers. Stars with a fine micrometer control over their emotions (upward or downward) in professional matters seem to make no effort to maintain it outside the field, thereby engendering major living problems that could have been shut off with a well-timed shrug or a wink at the outset.

Very rarely do we find a superpro giving some nonprofessional matter the full treatment even when it concerns something that could indirectly profoundly affect his work, like choosing a wife. True enough, we have seen the young Brunel musing over such a problem, applying to it something —just a little—of the probing, calculating, stress-appraising, vibration-recording thoughtfulness that contributed to his success as an engineer. But the kind of treatment I have in mind is that which Kepler brought to bear when choosing a second wife—and even here, as we shall see, there were very special circumstances involved.

THE ASTRONOMER TAKES A WIFE

Kepler was forty-one at the time and already distinguished in his profession. Consequently there was no shortage of candidates—eleven of whom came under what really proved to be active consideration. Koestler quotes in *The Watershed* a long letter in which the astronomer describes in meticulous detail the process of elimination and selection that followed —a document showing "that he solved the problem . . . by much the same method by which he found the orbit of Mars: he committed a series of mistakes which might have proved fatal, but canceled out; and up to the last moment he failed to realize that he held the correct solution in his hands."

The first contender was a widow ("known to me and my first wife, and unmistakably recommended to me by her") so "what could have seemed more reasonable than that I, as a philosopher, past the peak of virility, at an age when passion is extinct, the body dried and softened by nature, should have married [her]?" The main reasons against it were apparently that the woman had two marriageable daughters; that her money was in the hands of a trustee; and that "though her body was strong, it was suspect of ill health because of her stinking breath."

The second contender was one of the widow's two daughters, both of whom had been offered. This girl was, he confesses, quite captivating in appearance, but "her education had been, as it became sufficiently clear, more splendid than it would be useful to me. She had been brought up in luxury that was above her station, also she was not of a sufficient age to run a household." And so (after submitting these reasons to the mother, who "did not seem pleased") on to the third.

This was another girl Kepler found physically attractive and who further commended herself by showing her affection for his orphaned children. But when he left them for a while in her care he pronounced it "a rash act, for later on I had to fetch them back at my own expense." And she gave him doubts about her likely constancy, having given her word to another man a year before and being willing to break it in Kepler's favor.

The fourth had only her "tall stature and athletic build"

against her and he would have been glad to marry her if the fifth hadn't happened to come into the picture. This was Susanna, whom in fact he did eventually choose. She wasn't in his opinion, as good as the fourth "as regards the reputation of the family, earnestness of expression, property, and dowry"—but she had the advantage "through her love, and her promise to be modest, thrifty, diligent, and to love her stepchildren." Then came complications:

While I was waging my long and heavy battle with this problem, I was waiting for the visit of Frau Helmhard, wondering whether she could advise me to marry the third, who would then carry the day over the last-mentioned two. Having at last heard what this woman had to say, I began to decide in favor of the fourth, annoyed that I had to let the fifth go. As I was turning this over, and on the point of making a decision, fate intervened: the fourth got tired of my hesitations and gave her word to another suitor. Just as I had been previously annoyed about having to reject the fifth, I was now so much hurt about the loss of the fourth that the fifth too began to lose her attraction for me.

(To which he had at least the grace—and professional candor —to add: "In this case, to be sure, the fault was in my feelings.")

The sixth was another young girl, this time recommended by his stepdaughter (his first wife having been married previously). This contender had "a certain nobility, and some possessions" to further recommend her; "on the other hand, she was not old enough, and I feared the expense of a sumptuous wedding; and her noble rank in itself made her suspect of pride." Besides, he began to feel pity for Number Five, who had come to know what was afoot. So he switched back to Susanna, only to be distracted almost at once by the claims put forward for a seventh contender by people who "suspected the humility of the fifth" and recommended the newcomer's noble rank. She too was a good-looker and again he was prepared to give up the fifth "and to choose the seventh, provided it was true what they said about her . . ." But once more he hesitated, thereby bringing about his rejection by the seventh—a rejection which (he had the sense to realize and the honesty to confess) he had himself "quasi-provoked."

People were now gossiping. To still their tongues and turn aside their ridicule, he passed on to a candidate of common origin "who nevertheless aspired to the nobility," and whose mother "was a most worthy person." But she was plain, and fickle, giving and retracting her word no fewer than seven times, and he proceeded to the ninth.

With this one he was very devious. She had a lung disease but was otherwise very attractive, and to test her feelings he pretended to be in love with someone else. She reacted by telling her mother, whose own reaction was to give him her blessing, but Kepler mistakenly thought he'd been rejected and went on to the tenth: a woman of noble rank, ample means, thrifty, but very ugly. The ugliness was decisive. Kepler moved on to Number Eleven: again a noblewoman, wealthy, and thrifty. But after waiting four months for an answer, only to be told that she wasn't yet old enough, Kepler went back to the fifth and remained there.

As Koestler points out, Kepler's total immersion in the problem is strangely reminiscent "of the method of his scientific discoveries." And it was equally successful. "Susanna seemed to have justified Kepler's choice, and lived up to his expectations. There is hardly any later mention of her in his letters, and as far as Kepler's domestic life was concerned, no news is good news." But what really concerns us here is this: that Kepler was probably only able to apply that total immersion technique because the search for a wife coincided with a sudden slacking off in his professional affairs, after the abdication of his imperial patron, Rudolph, and Kepler's move from Prague to a much humbler job and semi-exile in provincial Linz.

THE NOVELIST ADVISES A SISTER

As I have already said, such a transference of application is very rare indeed. More often a superprofessional will be able to give sound advice, based on his professional experience or instincts, about *somebody else's* everyday problems or ambitions. Here, for instance, is the still young Scott Fitzgerald positively ladling it out to his kid sister, Annabel, who was pretty but rather retiring:

You are as you know, not a good conversationalist and you might very naturally ask "What do boys like to talk about?" Boys like to talk about themselves—much more than girls. Here are some leading questions for a girl to use. . . . (a) You dance so much better than you did last year. (b) How about giving me that sporty necktie when you're thru with it? (c) You've got the longest eyelashes! (This will embarrass him, but he likes it.) (d) I hear you've got a "line"! (e) Well who's your latest crush? *Avoid* (a) When do you go back to school? (b) How long have you been home? (c) It's warm or the orchestra's good or the floor's good . . .

As you get a little older you'll find that boys like to talk about such things as smoking and drinking. Always be very liberal—boys hate a pry—tell them you don't object to a girl smoking but don't like cigarettes yourself. Tell them you smoke only cigars—Kid them! . . . Never try to give a boy the affect that you're popular—Ginevra always starts by saying she's a poor unpopular woman without any beaux. Always pay close attention to the man. Look at him in his eyes if possible. Never affect boredom. It's terribly hard to do it gracefully. Learn to be worldly. Remember in all society nine out of ten girls marry for money and nine men out of ten are fools. . . .

§ 163 §

Expression, that is facial expression, is one of your weakest points. A girl of your good looks and at your age ought to have almost perfect control of her face. It ought to be almost like a mask. . . . (a) A good smile and one that could be assumed at will, is an absolute necessity. You smile on one side which is *absolutely wrong*. Get before a mirror and practice a smile and get a good one, a "radiant smile" ought to be in the facial vocabulary of every girl. Practice it—on girls, on the family. Practice doing it when you don't feel happy and when you're bored. When you're embarrassed, when you're at a disadvantage. That's when you'll have to use it in society and when you've practiced a thing in calm, then only are you sure of it as a good weapon in tight places. (b) A laugh isn't so important but it's well to have a good one on ice. Your natural one is very good, but your artificial one is bum. Next time you laugh naturally remember it and practice so you can do it any time you want. *Practice anywhere.* (c) A pathetic appealing look is one every girl ought to have . . . it's best done by opening the eyes wide and drooping the mouth open a little, looking inward (hanging the head a little) directly into the eyes of the man you're talking to. Ginevra and Sandra use this when getting off their "I'm so unpopular" speeches and indeed they use it about half the time. Practice this. (d) Don't bite or twist your lips—it's sure death for any expression. (e) The two expressions *you* have control over now are no good. One is the side smile and the other is the thoughtful look with the eyes half closed. I'm telling you this because mother and I have absolutely no control over our facial expressions and we miss it. . . .

With such splendid eyebrows as yours you should brush them or wet them and train them every morning and night as I advised you to do long ago. They oughtn't to have a hair out of place. . . . I noticed last Saturday that your gestures are awkward and so unnatural as to seem affected. Notice the way graceful girls hold their hands and feet. How they stoop, wave, run and then try because you can't practice these things when men are around. It's too late then. They ought to be incentive then . . .

You see if you get anywhere and feel you look alright then there's one worry over and one bolt shot for self-confidence . . .

TWO OBSTACLES

It would be interesting to know if Annabel followed up her brother's advice. One can easily see why she might not have, excellent though it was, with its notes on maximizing assets, eradicating deficiencies, learning from mistakes, controlling emotions, and attending to detail. And if she did let it slide, the reason for such failure would only be precisely the same as the one which later kept Scott Fitzgerald himself from applying such deep, thought-consuming, detailed attention to his own, much greater nonprofessional problems. Quite simply, there are other things to do in life. In his case there were bills to meet, a mentally sick wife to cope with, a comeback to make. Had he devoted to the attack on his alcoholism the same dedication and single-mindedness he gave to his writing talent, had he applied himself in such detail exclusively to that problem, relegating everything else, including his writing, to the background for a substantial period of time, he might have solved it much earlier and more conclusively than he did.

Here then are two of the greatest obstacles to the application of the qualities we have been discussing to everyday living: (1) the need for single-mindedness in pursuit of an object; and (2) the closely linked need for a sufficiently strong desire to attain that object—a desire that has to power the dedication and keep it powered throughout the pursuit. The trouble is that if the single-mindedness and the powering desire sustaining it are strong enough, the field of operation then ceases to be "everyday" in the usual meaning of the term. It becomes virtually a professional area in its own right, with, say, the girl becoming a professional husband-catcher and the writer a professional abstainer. Similarly, the canned-meat salesman who adapts the superprofessional attitudes and techniques to gaining promotion is in danger of becoming that greatest of all bores: the man who "lives, sleeps, and eats" canned meats, or whatever other mundane lines he might be specializing in.

Failure fully to appreciate these factors seems to me to be the great weakness in educational thinking on the subject of excellence generally. On the one hand we have the traditional biographical approach, heavily studded with colorful anecdotes, and on the other we have modern experiments in motivational training, equally heavily besprinkled with psychosociological jargon. In the first case the student is presented with the exhortation direct: "Model yourself on him and you too can make it" or, negatively, "Why can't *you* be like that?" In the second case the student is subjected to a battery of techniques designed to stimulate a desire for excellence and provide him at the same time with the means—a kind of handy strategy-kit—to attain it. Among these means, various familiar items keep cropping up: like the assessment and handling of mistakes through feedback, and the supersaturation bombardment of detail in brainstorming sessions. But what is usually missing is singleness of mind.

This is an understandable omission. Schools and colleges have curriculums and for a student to throw himself with wholehearted passion into any one subject could very easily cause him to do only moderately well or downright badly with the others. (In this connection one thinks of the boy Dylan Thomas—always top student in English, always bottom in everything else.) And yet, will a student attain excellence without that single-mindedness? Faced with this dilemma, the experimentalists tend to back off. The "planning to attain excellence" becomes a planning to achieve modest self-selected goals: to improve one's grades to a merely pass-able level, to get a vacation job, to save a little money. Thus a go-cart is hitched to a Cadillac engine, the *desire* for excel-lence.

The result of this muddled thinking on the part of the experimenters is—as far as one can judge from some of the published interviews with students—an even greater be-wilderment in the minds of the subjects. Yet even this is not as bad as the effect that the initial whipping up of a desire to achieve, to succeed, to attain excellence, might have on certain students. Suppose the desire escalates into a lust? And suppose the lust cannot be adequately supported by talent or basic skill? How does one in fact make use of the proven methods of a pantheon of moral or emotional cripples, anti-social brooders, ruthless privateers, and egomaniacs—which in one shape or another is what most superpros are—without creating, through the powerful and *indispensable* emotional element, additional misfits, who lack the saving grace of talent and the massive compensations that fully exploited talent can bestow on humanity at large?

Some supporters and upholders of traditional educa-tional methods will no doubt be wondering what else but a dangerous muddle of this kind is to be expected from modern experimentalists. But the point is that what the latter are doing in this case is no more than a logical extension of the time-honored pedagogical extolment and exemplification of Great Men and Women (in History, in Literature, in Sci-ence, et al.). One quails to think of the avalanches of bio-graphical snow jobs—selective to the point of stark dishonesty —that have been heaped on the backs of generations of chil-dren in every part of the world, with instructions to go and do likewise. And of the difficulties, disappointments, and disasters brought about by a blind obedience to this injunc-tion. And of the oceans of cheap cynicism generated in the hearts of those who managed to evade or extricate themselves from such predicaments. Now at last there are some teachers who, in putting the matter to the test in the classroom, are getting down to the particularities involved and, as a direct if totally unexpected result, are revealing the enormity of past mistakes.

The shade of Niccolò di Bernardo Machiavelli might be permitted an austere smile.

Works
Consulted

BELLOW, SAUL, *Henderson the Rain King*
BRODIE, FAWN M., *The Devil Drives*
BRYANT, ARTHUR, *Nelson*
CALLAS, EVANGELIA, *My Daughter—Maria Callas*
DE QUINCEY, THOMAS, *Recollections of the Lakes and the Lake Poets*
ELLMANN, RICHARD, *James Joyce*
FITZGERALD, BRIAN, *Daniel Defoe: A Study in Conflict*
FLESCH, CARL, *The Art of Violin Playing, Book One; The Art of Violin Playing, Book Two*
FREUD, SIGMUND, *Leonardo da Vinci and a Memory of his Childhood*
GRAHAM, SHEILAH, *Scratch an Actor*

HARRIS, KENNETH, "Piggott" (interview with Lester Piggott reported in *Observer*, London, 7 June 1970)

HYDE, H. MONTGOMERY, *Henry James at Home*

JONES, ERNEST, *The Life and Work of Sigmund Freud*

KENNEDY, MICHAEL, *Barbirolli: Conductor Laureate*

KOESTLER, ARTHUR, *The Act of Creation; The Watershed*

KNEPLER, HENRY, *The Gilded Stage*

LESLIE, C. R., *Memoirs of the Life of John Constable, Esq., R.A.*

MACHIAVELLI, *The Discourses* (Bernard Crick, ed.)

MAJESKI, BILL, "Easy as Rolling Off a Monologue" (article in *The New York Times*, 1 August 1971)

MANN, THOMAS, *Confessions of Felix Krull, Confidence Man*

MATTHEISSEN, F. O., *Henry James, The Major Phase*

MATTHEISSEN, F. O. (with Kenneth B. Murdock) (ed.), *The Notebooks of Henry James*

MCKNIGHT, GERALD, *Verdict on Schweitzer*

NICOLLE, JACQUES, *Louis Pasteur: A Master of Scientific Inquiry*

Official Transcript, *Trial of the Chicago Seven*

POPE-HENNESSY, UNA, *Charles Dickens*

REWALD, JOHN, *Paul Cézanne*

ROLT, L. T. C., *Isambard Kingdom Brunel*

SCOTT, TOM (with Geoffrey Cousins), *Golf Secrets of the Masters*

SIMENON, GEORGES, *Maigret's Mistake*

SINGER, KURT, *The Danny Kaye Saga*

STANISLAVSKI, CONSTANTIN, *My Life in Art*

STEVENSON, ROBERT LOUIS, "The Art of Writing"

THOMAS, PIRI, *Down These Mean Streets*

TIDYMAN, ERNEST, *Shaft's Big Score*

TORRES, JOSÉ, *Sting Like a Bee*

TOWNSEND, ROBERT, *Up the Organization*

TURNBULL, ANDREW, *Scott Fitzgerald*

WARNER, OLIVER, *Trafalgar*

WHARTON, EDITH, *A Backward Glance*

WILENSKI, R. H., *English Painting*

WOODHAM-SMITH, CECIL, *Florence Nightingale*

Index